by the same author

JUST BACK FROM GERMANY

MY HOST MICHEL

LORD HAW-HAW—AND WILLIAM JOYCE

THE VIEW FROM THE PEAK

Prince of Spies

Major Henri Le Caron

Prince of Spies

Henri Le Caron

J.A. COLE

faber and faber
LONDON·BOSTON

First published in 1984
by Faber and Faber Limited
3 Queen Square London WC1N 3AU
Typeset by Goodfellow & Egan Limited
Printed in Great Britain by
Ebenezer Baylis & Sons Limited, Worcester

© *J. A. Cole, 1984*

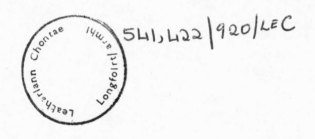

British Library Cataloguing in Publication Data

Cole, J. A.
Prince of spies.
1. Le Caron, Henri   2. Espionage—Ireland
I. Title
327.1'2'0924   HV7961

ISBN 0-571-13233-2

Library of Congress Data has been applied for.

Contents

Illustrations

Acknowledgements

I thank Anthony George Powell (fellow writer and BBC colleague) for suggesting a biography of Henri Le Caron—a generous gesture when he might have appropriated the idea for himself; Norman Evans, of the Public Record Office, London, for scholarly counsel, making documents available and reading the manuscript; Jean-Marie LeBlanc (Chief, Research and Inquiries, Manuscript Division), Michel Gauvin and Peter DeLottinville of the Public Archives of Canada for the loan of microfilm, suggestions as to sources, and the reproduction of a letter in Le Caron's handwriting; and Gordon Phillips, Archivist and Researcher of *The Times*, for Le Caron's portrait and press material.

J.A.C.

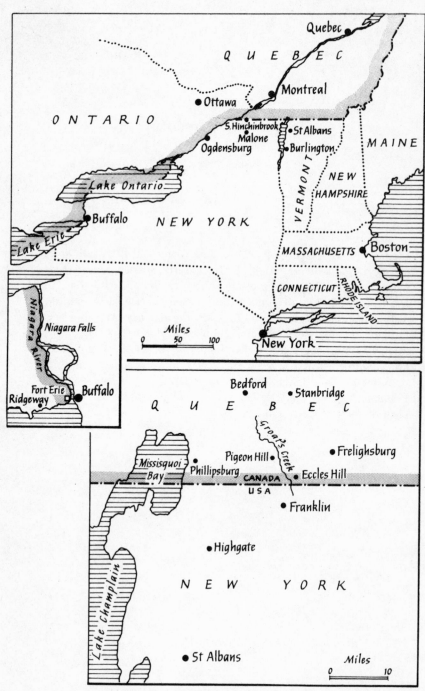

The area of the Fenian military operations

1

The Invaders

Among a mass of alarming news about an impending invasion, the *Ottawa Citizen* of 26 May 1870 printed this telegram under a New York by-line: 'The officers in command of the present raid are Gen. O'Neill, Col. Donnely, Col. Lewis, Col. Clingen and Col. Lecaron.'

Newspapermen were trying to compose a coherent account of the situation as an armed force of Irish-Americans attacked Canada. The main events they covered very well but a generation was to pass before they learned the real story which was concealed in a little-noticed name in that one brief paragraph. If they had discovered what was happening behind the scenes, they would have confronted the dilemma of a scoop that no responsible editor should have published.

The words 'the present raid' in the telegram were used because there had been a previous one. To introduce the characters involved, and to show how they came to be where they were, it is convenient to go back five years.

A convention in Cincinnati, Ohio, in September 1865, of the newly formed Senate Wing of the Fenian Brotherhood, an American-Irish organization dedicated to winning by force the independence of Ireland from British rule, decided that the prospects for a successful armed rebellion in Ireland were hopeless. This conclusion was arrived at, with much bitterness, after the 'Movement of '65'—a projected rising on Irish soil—collapsed and was seen to have been based on illusions fostered by two eloquent orators from the Irish

Revolutionary Brotherhood in Ireland, James Stephens and John O'Mahony. Stephens, the top man in the organization, bore the title 'Head Centre' (the local branches were known as 'centres'); his companion was billed as 'General'. Ranks and titles abounded in the Irish republican movement, and from now on they will be printed without inverted commas. This couple had gone to their counterpart in America (founded, as was their own society, in 1858) to raise men, money and arms to reinforce (they said) an existing army of disciplined men which was waiting only for this extra assistance to drive the British out of Ireland.

Irish eloquence is unmatched but had the visitors been no more than mildly persuasive they would have been assured of an ardent response. Audiences included immigrants who had left Ireland because of the potato famine of the late 1840s, their children, and later arrivals seeking in America a life of greater promise. The Irish population of America was already well over 1.5 million. As new-comers they had not arrived ignorant of the language, bearing unpronounceable names, and bewildered by the customs of an alien society; with their advantages they quickly established themselves. They retained their Irish character, their communal sense being fostered by their own clubs, churches and newspapers, as well as by their continuing ties with relatives back in the motherland, to whom they transmitted considerable sums of money. Living as they were in a country which had won its independence by armed revolt against British rule, they were easily open to persuasion that Ireland, with some help, could do the same. Crowd excitement, traditional songs and a good deal of drink had primed audiences even before the speeches started, and afterwards the money rolled in. Inevitably, Stephens and O'Mahony enjoyed a successful trip. Their tour of the principal American cities, where crowds greeted them with wild enthusiasm, netted $200,000, and a very large quantity of arms was assembled. All that remained was to establish the eager volunteers on the supposedly receptive Irish soil. A ship named the *Erin's Hope* was chartered and loaded with enough rifles, ammunition and other material for its occupants and the rebels waiting across the Atlantic. Other would-be liberators, who had failed to secure a place on the *Erin's Hope*, bought tickets for regular passenger ships. The plan was to land the *Erin's Hope* volunteers and cargo at night in a quiet bay on the west coast of Ireland, but while the ship was still at sea it was

14

intercepted by a British naval craft; without even a token resistance it was seized, the cargo confiscated, and everyone on board taken prisoner. Many fare-paying travellers arriving at ports were arrested as they walked down the gangplank. The disciplined army supposed to be awaiting these reinforcements proved to be a phantom.

Although the routine allegation that British spies had betrayed the plan was put into circulation, it was plainly not British spies who had stumped America making misleading speeches, raising money which was to be senselessly dissipated, and landing well-wishers in prison. So intense were the feelings aroused by this costly fiasco that the Fenian movement in the United States split, leaving Stephens and O'Mahony with only a minority of supporters.

Thus, in the aftermath of humiliating failure, there assembled in Cincinnati, under a new leader, Colonel William R. Roberts of New York, that convention which decided to keep the revolutionary movement alive by a spectacular action to be undertaken soon. A more accessible part of the British Empire was to be seized and from there the independence of Ireland negotiated. The slogan was: 'On to Canada'.

The delegates were in the mood for grand gestures. Losing no time, they adopted the plausible device of a government in exile. Purporting to be the Government of the Irish Republic, it assumed the features of a genuine regime. Its constitution copied that of the United States, and its documents in type and layout were indistinguishable at a glance from official publications. Colonel Roberts became President and General T. W. Sweeny (then commanding the 16th United States Infantry stationed at Nashville, Tennessee) was Secretary of War. Other ministers held appropriate titles. Money was raised by the issue of bonds, impressively engraved, to be repaid when the republic was established on Irish soil. Contributions again poured in in response to the impassioned speeches made at meetings and widely reported in newspapers.

Irishmen had fought on both sides in the American civil war. Now these veterans, along with eager new recruits, drilled openly as Irish army units, unhampered by the United States authorities who should have invoked the neutrality laws in accordance with their treaty with Canada. Edwin M. Stanton, the United States Secretary of War, was not averse to seeing the British Government embarrassed. During the civil war Britain had permitted the *Alabama* and other vessels to be built for the south in British shipyards; as these ships preyed on northern shipping, the American Government held that it was entitled to claim compensation for a British infringement of neutrality. Stanton looked forward to the ultimate annexation of Canada and he was willing to let the Irish see what they could do in the way of disruption. The Fenians were permitted to purchase war material, even from the United States Government, and General Sweeny made his plans in the knowledge that he would not be disciplined or encounter official opposition.

An Irishman with plenty of battle experience was appointed in charge of the assault. He was John O'Neill, born in 1834 in Clontibret, County Monaghan, and taken by his parents to America, where they settled at Elizabeth, New Jersey. At 23 he enlisted as a cavalryman. His first three years of service were spent fighting Red Indians in the far west. On the outbreak of the civil war he became a lieutenant in the 5th Indiana Cavalry, and as the war proceeded he was further promoted on transfer to an infantry regiment. Now demobilized, he was working in Nashville as a United States Claims Agent.

In his devotion to the Fenian cause, as in his war service, O'Neill proved himself a leader. Physically he had the advantage of being tall and of distinctive appearance; his vibrant voice charmed audiences. Reports of his often very long speeches reveal that he could draw up a good prospectus. When Ireland became independent and took her rightful place among the nations of the world, he assured excited crowds, industries would prosper in her valleys and the sails of foreign merchant ships crowd her harbours. No attempt was made to conceal the purpose of his fund-raising campaign.

Although it was apparent to the Canadian authorities that an invasion was being prepared, they had a 1,000-mile frontier and a scattered population of 4 million to defend. Some British regular troops were always on duty in Canada, but the volunteer militia in the provinces constituted the main force. Any attack was likely to meet with initial success.

O'Neill achieved the surprise he had planned. At about 3 a.m. on 1 June 1866 some 800 men under his command were towed in flat-bottomed boats by a steam tug across the Niagara River. An hour later they landed unopposed at a spot called Waterloo. Colonel Owen Starr, commanding the Kentucky contingent, planted the

Fenian flag on Canadian soil, and led his men forward into Ontario. As they advanced, however, their numbers dwindled. Some were attracted by the opportunities of loot in the undefended countryside, while others simply slipped away and made their way back to Buffalo, New York.

The remainder occupied a small place with the important-sounding name of Fort Erie. Their numbers were down to about 500, but they pushed on for a few miles to Ridgeway, where they found themselves opposed by the 22nd Battalion of Volunteers of Toronto. Quite a brisk fight took place here. At first the Fenians drove the volunteers back, but after some disorder the Canadians rallied and forced the invaders to retreat to Fort Erie. Nearly 200 continued the with-drawal, embarked in small boats, and returned to the United States side, leaving sixty dead. The rest, fearing themselves now greatly outnumbered by the Canadians, followed at 2 a.m. on 3 June. As they were being towed across the river they were hailed by the United States armed steamer *Michigan* and taken prisoner.

Back in Buffalo news of the capture of Fort Erie aroused such enthusiasm that an estimated 30,000 supporters assembled. They were not to cross the frontier. President Andrew Johnson belatedly invoked the neutrality laws, and the Fenians' weapons were seized by the American commander in Buffalo. General Sweeny disarmed his force, and he and O'Neill were arrested and put on bail. The men captured by the *Michigan* were bound over in their own recognizances and sent home.

One of the worst results, from the Fenian viewpoint, was that it exposed the movement to ridicule by the American and British press. The *New York Times* described the Fenians as 'a wretched-looking lot, totally deficient in uniform, and composed of the roughest-looking specimens of humanity'. The paper commented:

> If there is one thing that we Americans have prayed earnestly for since these bandit gangs were first formed, it was that every ruffian that crossed the frontier might be straightway caught and hung. The prospect of this was a sort of compensation for the intolerable nuisance of being obliged to listen to their blather day after day.

A letter to the London *Times* from James M'Cullam, of 73 Kensington Gardens Square, London W., put the capture of Fort Erie into perspective and at the same time advertised a desirable site:

Sir, By the recent arrival from America it is stated the Fenians have crossed Niagara River into Canada and captured Fort Erie with a small village in the rear. It may relieve the anxiety of people to know that Fort Erie, which belongs to me, consists of a corn mill and dwellinghouse and a few acres of land on the Canadian side of the Niagara. The corn mill was burnt a few years ago and the whole consists of a desirable site for a railway station when the proposed International bridge to Buffalo is built, but is worthless as a post for the Fenians or for any other belligerent.

In a lengthy comment *The Times* used such phrases as 'this foolish and criminal enterprise', 'a mere band of robbers and murderers', 'this miserable act of brigandage'; ignoring the President's delay, it added an appreciative note about the United States Government's action: 'We are almost disposed to thank the Fenians for having given the Americans an occasion for displaying so conspicuously their friendliness and good feeling.'

The *Illustrated London News* was no less forthright:

The Fenians have made a dash into Canada. A body of these demented creatures, under Colonel O'Neil [sic], variously estimated at from 500 to 2,000 strong, crossed Niagara river. . . . A fight has taken place between them and the Canadian volunteers. The affair was, however, a mere skirmish, and led to no decisive result. Several regiments of regulars were moving on the Fenians, and, it was expected, would capture the whole force.

A week later the magazine dismissed the affair:

The Fenian raid on Fort Erie . . . proved a complete failure, the whole band of invaders having been either captured by the Canadians or taken prisoners in their retreat by the Federal boats. . . . It was rumoured that there was to be a general rising of the Irish in Canada on the 7th, and the authorities had recourse to the usual expedient of suspending the Habeas Corpus Act; but, so far from an insurrection taking place, the Irish population, we are told, displayed an unexpected degree of loyalty.

General O'Neill's report to the Fenian President Roberts was scarcely less scathing than the accounts in the hostile press, except for its element of self-justification. As his immediate reaction it deserves quoting because receding time produced ever more heroic versions of the operation.

Here truth compels me to make an admission I would fain have kept from the public. Some of the men who crossed over with us the night before (i.e. the morning of the 1st of June) managed to leave the command during the day, and re-crossed to Buffalo, while others remained in the houses around the fort marauding. (Real Irish patriots these!) This I record to their lasting disgrace.

On account of this shameful desertion, and the fact that arms had been sent out for 800 men, I had to destroy 300 stand to prevent them from falling into the hands of the enemy. . . .

At this time I could not depend upon more than 500 men, one-tenth of the reputed number of the enemy, which I knew was surrounding me—rather a critical position.

Thus situated, and not knowing what was going on elsewhere, I decided that the best course was to return to Fort Erie and ascertain if crossings had been made at other points; and, if so, I was content to sacrifice myself and my noble little command for the sake of leaving the way open.

I returned to the old fort (Erie), and about six o'clock sent word to Captain W. J. Hynes, and his friends at Buffalo, that the enemy would surround me with 5,000 men before morning, fully provided with artillery; that my little command, which had by this time considerably decreased, could not hold out long; but that, if a movement was going on elsewhere, I was perfectly willing to make the old fort a slaughter-pen, which I knew would be the case the next day if I remained.

Previous to this time, some of the officers and men, realizing the danger of their position, availed themselves of the small boats and re-crossed the river; but the greater portion of them—317, including officers—remained until 2 a.m. June 3rd, when all, except a few wounded men, went safely on board a large scow attached to a tug-boat, and were hauled into American waters.

Here they were hailed by the United States steamer, which fired across their bows and demanded their surrender. With this request we complied, not because we feared the twelve-pounders or the still more powerful guns of the *Michigan*, but because we respected the authority of the United States.

19

Defeat, however abysmal, did not quench the Fenians' ardour. When they supported this enterprise they not only put out of their minds the *Erin's Hope* expedition but a previous adventure when they had set out to seize a small island called Campo Bello in the Bay of Fundy, where the United States frontier runs between Maine and New Brunswick, in the hope of provoking a territorial dispute between Britain and America; naval vessels of both powers peacefully prevented their landing, and they returned home having incurred expenses of $40,000.

Within quite a short time the record of the brief invasion of Canada was rewritten. Fund-raising was not stimulated by recalling past failures. The battle of Ridgeway became part of the mythology of the Fenian movement; its veterans boasted as though they had been present at one of the decisive battles of history, and orators claimed the encounter as a victory. A painting of the battle was exhibited at meetings and a book entitled *Ridgeway* appeared; in advertisements in the Irish-American press it was described as 'an interesting historical romance' and readers were promised a full recital of the wrongs of Ireland and a complete biography of General O'Neill. On the Canadian side, too, the participants did not see it, as have some more distant commentators, as a slight skirmish; to local inhabitants the attack was an outrage which aroused fierce emotions. Three student militiamen who fell were commemorated by a memorial window at University College, Toronto.

The two sides reached opposite conclusions. In Canada the efficacy and loyalty of the new dominion's volunteers were seen to have been established. The Fenians came to regard the raid as a rehearsal for a more ambitious military operation. They wanted another fight and it became O'Neill's mission to prepare for it.

2

The General's Confidant

In Nashville O'Neill moved in the company of war veterans to whom he talked freely of the project to repeat the assault on Canada. Preparations were to be secret, as the Fenians kept reminding themselves, but men cannot be enlisted for an action unless they are told about it. Inevitably, being gregarious and a good talker, he expressed his passionate desire to drive the British out of Ireland to anyone who would listen. One of his acquaintances, whom he had met in the army in 1864 and to whom he took a particular liking, was an ex-officer named Henri Le Caron, now living in Nashville.

O'Neill knew Le Caron as a Frenchman who had come to America to fight on the northern side in the civil war and who had decided to settle there. From the start he found him a sympathetic listener and an agreeable companion. All he knew about this man was his war record and it never seems to have occurred to him to inquire into his background. Nor did anybody else ever investigate him.

This is puzzling. Did not the local post office staff in Nashville notice that this Frenchman conducted a regular correspondence with England and little with France? The Fenians were accustomed to blame British spies for the failure of any of their enterprises, and their circulars contained routine warnings to members to look out for spies. Were there no Irish republican sympathizers handling the mail? Was there no neighbourly inquisitiveness about him? Certainly immigrants were streaming into America from every European country and there was nothing odd about a Frenchman living in Tennessee, but he never seems to have associated with other French nationals or to have exchanged youthful reminiscences as part of day-to-day friendly gossip.

The man known as Le Caron was in fact English, the son of John Joseph Billis Beach and Maria Beach, *née* Passmore. Born in Colchester, Essex, on 26 September 1841, the second son in what was to become a family of thirteen children, he was named Thomas Billis. At that time his father was a cooper, an occupation which accorded ill with his strict Methodism. This anomaly was later corrected when he became a rate collector.

Obviously the boy had some early education, but Thomas did not think it worth mentioning in the few accounts he gave of himself. Somehow he learned to write well enough to obtain employment as a clerk. He was small, agile and sharp-featured; his nature, according to his own description, was wild and exuberant. It is evident that he was impulsive. At the age of 12—perhaps finding home becoming overcrowded by the rapidly increasing family—he packed such essentials as his marbles and toys, slipped out of the house early one morning, and set out to walk to London. This episode should have taught him the importance of keeping his mouth shut at crucial times. Before he had gone far he met a schoolfellow to whom he confided his project. In no time his parents were on his track.

Colchester, with its garrison and market, must have had a certain liveliness to distinguish it from the surrounding villages. Yet Thomas sensed that elsewhere a different kind of life was possible. A second attempt to get away resulted in a fortnight's freedom. Then his father, in a drastic endeavour to tie him down, made one of those grotesque parental miscalculations which are the fate of unusual children by apprenticing him for seven years to the drapery trade. Thomas spent eleven months behind the counter of a shop in the High Street. His demeanour may be guessed from the fact that by then his employer, a Quaker named Thomas Knight, was glad to release him from the terms of his apprenticeship. At 16, through the help of relatives, he reached London at last, where his employment as a clerk in a drapery firm, Brooks & Company, in the Borough, was soon terminated because he accidentally set fire to the premises. Although not wanting him around any more, they found him another and better job with Olney & Company, Bucklersbury, but he soon gave this up and took a trip to Bath and Bristol. Of this expedition he merely writes that in Bristol he was 'struck down with a fever and reduced to a penniless condition'. Struggling back to

London on foot, he crawled into St Bartholomew's Hospital. Put into a bed next to a dying patient, whose agonies so frightened him that he discharged himself, he returned to his native town, gained admission to the Colchester and East Essex Institution, and stayed there until he recovered. Another brief term of employment followed with William Baber, described in the local paper as a tradesman.

At this stage of his career he looked like a ne'er-do-well but he was resourceful, energetic, and—a not inconsiderable quality—sober. Even on festive occasions Joseph Beach allowed no alcohol in his house, and this early training in abstinence was to give Thomas an advantage over the heavy drinkers with whom he frequently associated. 'When others lost their heads, and their caution as well,' he reflected after his retirement, 'I was enabled, through my distaste for drink, to benefit in every way.'

His next impulse took him, in 1859, to Paris. Apparently it was a random choice but it was a fairly obvious one. Paris was glamorous, easily accessible, and, with the many British and American businesses operating there, it offered opportunities of employment. None the less, the move required considerable spirit, because he had no friends there and no knowledge of the language. Another essential quality for the adventurer now appeared—luck. He put up at an hotel kept by an Englishwoman in the Faubourg St-Honoré and eked out his money while he explored the city. Just as his cash was running low he happened one Sunday to pass the little English church in the rue d'Aguesseau while a service was being held. The sound of his own language is a powerful lure to a lonely stroller in a foreign town. He entered and joined in the familiar hymns. The appearance of this newcomer attracted attention. While the congregation lingered chatting after the service, the incumbent, the Reverend Dr Forbes, persuaded him to become a member of the choir. He left the church in the company of an Englishman who was so interested in his story that he found a place in his lodging for him, lent him money, and in a week introduced him to a job in Maison Withers, à la Suissesse, 52 Faubourg St-Honoré. Young Beach had a way of inspiring confidence and trust without being ingratiating. Dr Forbes eventually secured him a better position in the banking house of Arthur & Company.* Many of the firm's customers were Americans,

*Oddly enough, in 1879 Arthur & Company was the code name used inside the Fenian movement for the Irish Revolutionary (or Republican) Brotherhood.

and thus he made the acquaintance of the American colony in Paris.

This community was thrown into turmoil by the outbreak of the American civil war in April 1861. Customers closed their accounts; social gatherings became depleted as young men left for home. Recruiting appeals circulated offering contracts for three months; at the outset of a war people cannot imagine that it will last long. Thomas Beach, now aged 19, was caught up in the excitement. Obviously he had formed no attachment to keep him in Paris and he saw the chance of another escapade. Looking back, he described his decision as a joke. Another attraction must have been the opportunity of travelling on Brunel's *Great Eastern* on her first voyage to New York. Intending not to stay in America for long, he went there to join the northern army.

On making this move, from Europe to America, from civilian to soldier, he gave himself a new identity by adopting a false name and posing as French. His intention was, he explained later, to save his parents concern by concealing from them what he was doing, but how this scheme worked is not apparent. Possibly he felt that a French sympathizer was likely to be more acceptable to the Americans than an Englishman joining for no obvious motive. He was by no means the only recruit giving an assumed name; passports and identity cards did not then limit people's freedom to disown their past, and the new soldiers would have had all sorts of personal reasons for wanting to start a new life. It says a lot for Thomas Beach's self-confidence that he thought, after only two years in Paris, that he could become a convincing Frenchman. How well he spoke the language can be only a matter of conjecture. Much of Arthur & Company's business was in English and he would have learned no French among his American companions. But even in a wholly French environment it seems unlikely that, in two years, he could have become bilingual. Certainly he was not inhibited by instruction in French at school. People not conditioned to worry about irregular verbs and relative pronouns seem, in the right surroundings, to pick up a language at a speed astonishing to those who have undergone formal training, but it is rare for an Englishman to be able to pass as a Frenchman, or for a Frenchman to sound English.

A British policeman—judging by other evidence not a careful reporter—who came to know Thomas Beach twenty-eight years later quoted him as saying that he adopted the name Le Caron because he had been employed in a restaurant kept by a married couple of that name. Nowhere else is there any reference to this employment, but Beach might have said that he frequented such a restaurant. Whatever its origin, Henri Le Caron came into existence in New York on 7 August 1861, the day he enlisted in the 8th Pennsylvanian Reserves as a private.

When the three months for which he had signed up expired he decided to stay on for the duration. Soldiering had given him the break in his life pattern which he needed; the draper's shop and the counting-house desk were now abandoned for ever. His parents had to be told; they received his confession with dismay.

Soon he transferred to the Anderson Cavalry. During the Peninsula campaign of the Army of the Potomac he saw considerable action. In October 1862 his regiment joined the Western Army, and he attained non-commissioned rank.

In his autobiography (see Chapter 28) he gives little more than an outline of his military career and his references to battles in which he fought are as laconic as any routine military communiqué. His style becomes only slightly less stilted when he relates a romantic episode which might well, sixty or so years later, have provided the story-line of a Hollywood film script.

On Christmas Eve, 1862, he was in charge of a mounted party on reconnaissance. Without prearrangement the troop of thirty stopped at a house some 15 miles from Nashville, to rest their horses and eat. It was common practice, he writes, to quarter themselves in this way and to pay the residents for hospitality, so their reception was not grudging. Le Caron never suggests that the behaviour of the northern forces was other than impeccable.

While supper was being prepared he chatted agreeably with the owner's niece. It is characteristic of him that nowhere in his book does he mention her name. She was Nannie Melville, daughter of an Irish Virginian planter and a German mother. 'We were in fancied security,' he records, 'and gave no thought to immediate danger.' This looks like an admission that he had failed to take the elementary precaution of posting guards at points where they could sound an alarm if anyone approached. Half the troop were still outside with the horses but were not on the alert. 'In a moment, however, all was confusion. The house was suddenly surrounded by a band of

25

irregular troops, calling themselves Confederates, but in reality nothing more or less than marauders, and soon the fortunes of war were turned against us.'

The cavalrymen outside simply fled with the horses. Those in the house were overpowered and locked up in what he describes as a large log smoke-house. A guard was placed outside. The prisoners lay in the dark, listening to the raucous voices of the irregulars enjoying what was to have been their supper. Their position was desperate. Irregulars seldom gave quarter. If not massacred, they could be handed over to the southern forces and imprisoned.

Gradually the voices died away as their captors, replete, fell asleep. Now the owner's niece, disregarding the danger she might have to face the following morning, decoyed the guard away to have his supper. Then she returned, unbolted the door and let the prisoners out. Their horses having all gone, they walked 15 miles back to the camp. What explaining he had to do back at base he does not say; the incident clearly had no effect on his later promotion.

He did not meet his rescuer again until April 1864, when he was in camp in Nashville. Recommended for a commission, he was waiting to appear before a promotion board. Miss Melville was living with an aunt in Nashville, as the house where they met had been destroyed in the war. How the irregulars reacted on discovering their captives gone Le Caron does not relate, but evidently she suffered no harm. The scenario demanded that he should fall in love with his rescuer. During their courtship 'she, a bright-eyed daring horsewoman, and I, a happy-go-lucky cavalry officer, scampered the plains together in pleasant company.' This is the sole physical description he gives of her. The passage, however, hints at how he saw himself. Military service had transformed him from a civilian in a sedentary job to a cigar-smoking cavalry officer with the large moustache of his profession. He establishes his image in an anecdote which, considering his inhibited style of writing, occupies disproportionate space. Seeing a handsome black horse, he requisitioned it for army use. The result was a petition in several verses signed by the local women, explaining that to them the horse was a dear friend, their only means of transporting themselves and their loads, and appealing to the captain to return it. Le Caron, in the role of the gallant officer, yielded to this entreaty by the fair sex. Surely he smiled and twirled that moustache as he consented.

Le Caron was gazetted second lieutenant in the United States Army in July 1864. In the following December, while attached to General Stedman's division of the Army of the Cumberland, he took part in the battle of Nashville, and he was in all the engagements through Tennessee and Alabama, emerging from these as a first lieutenant. Further promotion soon followed and during 1865, the last year of the war, he held among other positions those of Acting Assistant Adjutant-General and Regimental Adjutant.

Throughout his army service he was only once seriously wounded. During an engagement near Woodbury, Tennessee, his horse was killed under him by a shell and he received a splinter which put him in hospital for a month. A companion at his side was killed.

On demobilization in February 1866 he joined the veteran organizations of the Army of the Cumberland and the Grand Army of the Republic, being listed as major. He chose to be known by this rank from then on.

The character of Major Le Caron was now completed. He was a man of some standing in the locality, married, with money in the bank. He had enjoyed the excitements the young Thomas Beach had craved, and he had acquired another ambition. He determined to become a doctor of medicine.

He described his regular letters to his father as written in 'the careless spirit of a wanderer's notes'. Yet those notes contained, among other gossip, an account of O'Neill and what the Fenians were up to.

3

Two Solemn Oaths

Were Le Caron's letters to his father merely the gossipy jottings which he later represented them to be? Did they not, in their accounts of conversations and revelation of plans, go beyond the normal contents of family correspondence? Was there no note of alarm, even of indignation, in what he wrote?

To the writer hardened by over four years of active service they would, admittedly, have seemed less dramatic than they did to a rate collector in peaceful Colchester, but John Beach was too stirred by them to keep their contents to himself. A simple patriot, he decided to warn the Government of this threat to the Empire. Perhaps the distant son had vaguely hoped that his father would be moved to action, but if this was his intention he was offering himself as an informer in a somewhat oblique manner.

Colchester was represented by two Members of Parliament, a Tory and a Liberal. As a Liberal supporter Beach approached John Gurdon Rebow with his son's letters. If they had been just the wanderer's notes which Le Caron claimed, the Member would have expressed polite thanks, assured the sender that he would forward them to the appropriate quarter, and left it to some Whitehall department to return them with a formal acknowledgement. Rebow was perceptive enough to see that they were no ordinary letters. He asked Beach's permission, which was eagerly given, to show them to the Home Secretary. Sir George Grey was sufficiently impressed to suggest that further correspondence should be shown to him and the writer asked to find out all he could of the Fenian plans.

Beach complied. He did not reveal the ultimate destination of his son's answers but Le Caron understood that his father was not simply motivated by personal curiosity. While he had no access to the Fenian higher councils, he picked up enough information to keep Rebow and the Home Secretary interested.

In 1867, still only 26, the runaway son paid his first visit home, where his father received him as a hero. Rebow invited them to his house, Wivenhoe Park, and he several times went to the Beach household. John Beach's gratification can be imagined. Le Caron told the Member all he knew which was, broadly, that the Fenian movement had swiftly recovered from its discouragement following the attack on Canada two years earlier, that it still had plentiful financial backing, and that it was planning a further adventure.

Le Caron guessed what was coming when Rebow asked his permission to discuss the matter in Whitehall, and he was not surprised, a few days later, to receive through Rebow a request to attend an interview in London. Two officials met him at 50 Harley Street, a private house where such talks could be discreetly conducted. They proposed that he should become a government agent and penetrate the Fenian organization. The young man accepted at once as (his own words): 'My adventurous nature prompted me to sympathy with the idea; my British instincts made me a willing worker from a sense of right, and my past success promised good things for the future.'

Judged by later standards, the arrangement was a casual one. He was not vetted, put through a training course, placed on contract with a service grade, an appropriate salary and a scale of expenses, instructed in codes and channels of communication. The only brief was to pick up what information he could and write, as before, to his father. He stipulated, and this was accepted, that the letters should remain his property; in other words, they would not be official documents beyond his retrieval. He did not argue about remuneration; that was regularized later. British consuls running networks of informants in the United States were not notified of his existence. He was to be on his own.

John Beach, who had chosen for his son the quiet life of a provincial draper, had now helped to launch him on a career of constant peril. The newly recruited agent knew enough of the Fenians to have no illusions about the danger of the work. Two of his brothers were in the army and he thought of himself as, like them, serving Queen and country.

An army surgeon, Dr Bacon, with whom Le Caron had been friendly during the war, assisted him to enter the Chicago Medical College and then (after about a year's study) took him on his own medical staff at the Illinois State Penitentiary. This institution, housing about 1,500 prisoners, was managed by three commissioners who ran the place as a private business. Prisoners able to pay exorbitant prices could buy any luxury at the commissioners' shop, contractors did deals to hire convict labour, releases were negotiated for money, and astute prisoners with financial resources manipulated their fellow inmates and the staff. 'A more quick-witted lot of men it has never been my fate to meet,' Le Caron recalled.

While advancing his medical studies in surroundings which afforded extensive and unusual experience, Le Caron embarked on his career in espionage. O'Neill, always a worthwhile target, was to become even more valuable. At the 1867 Cleveland Convention he was elected a senator of the Fenian Brotherhood, and on the resignation of Colonel Roberts, on the last day of that year, O'Neill succeeded him as President.

Meeting O'Neill in New York, Le Caron volunteered his services as a trained soldier in the event of any military action. The offer was gladly accepted and O'Neill promised him a responsible position. In the meantime, Le Caron undertook to help the cause.

Applicants for admission to the Fenian Brotherhood made this declaration: 'I solemnly pledge my sacred word of honour, as a truthful and honest man, that I will labour with earnest zeal for the liberation of Ireland from the yoke of England, and for the establishment of a free and independent government on the Irish soil.' There followed a list of rules and prohibitions in which 'carrying information to the enemy' came under the heading of 'Perfidy'.

Le Caron felt no twinge of conscience in giving his pledge. With the apparent zeal of a new supporter, he founded a Fenian circle, or camp, in Lockport, Illinois, and became its 'centre'. In this capacity he received all the reports, orders and other documents issued by O'Neill, and in his other role he transmitted their contents (sometimes even the originals) to England. Statements from Fenian headquarters were frequent and lengthy; when it was unsafe to let the papers out of his possession, he was committed—in those pre-typewriter days—to copying them by hand. Envelopes containing letters to his father became ever bulkier.

Within a few months he moved to the inside of Fenian affairs. While engaged at the hospital he received a telegram from O'Neill: 'Come at once, you are needed for work.' To comply meant resigning his post and interrupting his medical studies. The governor, who not unreasonably considered that Le Caron owed him a duty, offered him an increase in salary to persuade him to stay and, when this was refused, pressed for the reason. As he was unable to give a satisfactory explanation, Le Caron left on strained terms.

The Fenian Brotherhood headquarters to which he reported was in a mansion at 10 West Fourth Street, New York, where a staff performed duties as though they were the officials of an established government. Le Caron was handed a document bearing a coat of arms with a harp in the centre above the word 'Ireland' and beginning 'Know ye, That reposing special Trust and Confidence in the patriotism, valor, fidelity and abilities of Henri Le Caron he is hereby appointed Major and Military Organizer in the Service of the Irish Republic to rank as such from August 5th 1868.' It was signed on behalf of the War Department by John O'Neill. His salary was $60 a month with $7 a day expenses. He was assigned to proceed to the Eastern States with a civil organizer to inspect and reorganize Fenian military units.

The military wing of the Brotherhood required a more specific oath:

> I do solemnly swear before Almighty God that I will faithfully discharge my duty as a soldier of the Irish Republic against all enemies and opposers whomsoever, that I will faithfully and promptly obey all orders of the President of the Fenian Brotherhood and all officers of the same appointed over me, that I will observe the strictest secrecy in regard to all matters appertaining to the military movement and all orders that I may receive except to give such instructions to those under my charge or to whom I may be directed as shall enable them to perform their respective duties. I further pledge that in case of my being compelled by private duties to leave my present locality that I will feel myself bound under oath to join a branch of the military organization wherever I may

reside providing there is an opportunity and to report myself for duty whenever called upon. That I will consider the clothing, equipment and arms which I may use as a soldier of the Irish Republic as the property of the Fenian Brotherhood, so help me God.

This oath, too, Le Caron took without compunction. Although he allowed it to be assumed, in his guise as a Frenchman, that he was a Catholic, he did not believe in a deity. At some point in his journey from Colchester to America he had sloughed off the simple fervent Christianity of his parents and he felt no need of a religious faith.

A few hours after Le Caron was commissioned in the republican army, O'Neill appeared at a demonstration at Williamsburg, a suburb of Brooklyn, accompanied by the new major and other officers. A huge audience applauded the headquarters party as it filed on to the platform. As successive speakers were called upon Le Caron grew nervous; it was evident that his turn would come, he was no orator and he knew very little of Irish affairs. O'Neill had not yet spoken when Le Caron heard his own name uttered. By a happy slip of the tongue the chairman introduced him as Major M'Caron, and it was thus as an honorary Irishman that the National Organizer made his first speech. The reception accorded the other speakers had demonstrated that all an excited crowd wants to hear is a string of clichés, so he produced the expected platitudes and kept his address short by pleading that he did not wish to stand between them and the gallant hero of Ridgeway, General O'Neill. The hearty applause as he sat down convinced him 'that if it took so little as this to arouse the Irish people, I could play my role with but little difficulty'.

O'Neill's trust in Le Caron was such that he took him to a highly confidential interview with the President, Andrew Johnson. Their reception was cordial. Johnson, formerly Military Governor in Tennessee, had been friendly with O'Neill since 1862. O'Neill's purpose now was to secure the return of the Fenians' weapons seized by the American commander in Buffalo. Johnson, wanting the Irish vote and anxious to assure O'Neill of his sympathy, reminded the Fenian leader that he had delayed five days before taking any action, and declared: 'If you could not get there in five days, by God, you could never get there; and then, as President, I was compelled to enforce the Neutrality Laws, or be denounced on every side.'

The arms were returned to the Fenians on condition that they would not be used in any unlawful enterprise.

Le Caron transmitted such high-level intelligence to his father, who passed it on to his Member of Parliament. Then an alarming event occurred in London which resulted in the channel of communication being changed.

4

Alarm in London

Widespread repercussions resulted from an attempted prison rescue in London in December 1867. Held in the Clerkenwell House of Correction was an Irish-American Fenian colonel, Ricard Bourke (also spelt Burke), charged with the rescue of two men from a prison van in Manchester in September. The party to set him free in his turn was led by another Irish-American officer, Captain James Murphy, and it included Michael Barrett and Patrick Casey, whose brother Joseph was also in the prison awaiting trial.

Tipped off from Dublin, Scotland Yard issued a detailed warning of the plan 'to blow up the exercise walls by means of gunpowder' during the prisoners' afternoon exercise period, the signal to be a white ball thrown up outside. Watching police, concealed from view, saw men arrive with a cask on a barrow and light the fuse. Bourke, seeing the white ball, fell out of line and pretended to tie a bootlace. The flame, however, went out because the fuse was damp, and Bourke, realizing that something had gone wrong, rejoined the other prisoners. The would-be rescuers went away unmolested.

Unaware that the prison authorities had put the prisoners in a different yard, the party repeated the procedure the next day with a dry fuse and caused an explosion which not only damaged the wall but killed four people and injured forty in the houses opposite. Some Republican Brotherhood members were so horrified that they denounced the action that evening.

The astonishing police excuse, that they were misled by expecting the wall to be blown up whereas it was blown down, failed to allay public alarm, and the sense of outrage resulted in 50,000 men volunteering as special constables in London and double that number in the provinces. It was a disaster for the Fenians as it made them unpopular among the Irish in England, who felt their English neighbours' hostility, Barrett was hanged (it was the last public execution in England), and nothing was achieved. But other Irish revolutionaries, seeing the public commotion, were to be strengthened in their belief in the political power of dynamite.

Murphy and Patrick Casey escaped to Paris. The French Government refused a British request for extradition, and they were joined by Joseph Casey on his acquittal. The brothers, working as compositors, belonged to a group of Irish exiles on whom Scotland Yard kept an eye.

The placid offices in Whitehall were not easily aroused. Robert Anderson, a civil servant in the office of the Chief Secretary for Ireland, who in 1868 became Home Office adviser on matters relating to political crime, records that working hours in the Home Office were 11 a.m. to 5 p.m. and comments: 'It was a nominal 11 and a punctual 5.' But the Clerkenwell explosion alarmed the Government and continued to reverberate along Whitehall corridors. Reports from the United States, too, indicated that another attack on Canada was being planned. It was high time that the Government reviewed its sources of intelligence on the Fenian movement.

Fresh in their minds was a failure through carelessness. Robert Anderson had revealed to the Earl of Mayo, the Chief Secretary to the Lord-Lieutenant of Ireland, the name of an agent he was sending to America to penetrate the Fenian movement. Later, at the Viceregal Lodge in Dublin, the Earl and the Lord-Lieutenant were dining together and talking, no doubt, in the penetrating voices of the British upper class who scarcely acknowledged the existence of servants (or, indeed, of anybody else) except as the recipients of orders. The Earl told the Lord-Lieutenant who the agent was. Standing behind the screen covering the service door was an Irish servant. It would have been odd if the domestic staff at the Viceregal Lodge had not included persons with Fenian sympathies (even if they had not, as is highly probable, been planted there by the Irish Revolutionary Brotherhood). The name of the agent, and his mission, were reported in the servants' hall. Shortly after landing in New York the man was shot.

Under new arrangements which were now instituted, John Beach and Rebow ceased to be links in the chain of communication between Le Caron and London. In future letters were to be sent as from Nannie Le Caron to 'a lady relative' of Robert Anderson. The letters would remain, as before, Le Caron's property, to be returned to him on demand. Anderson, with the fate of his previous agent in mind, decided that nobody but himself would deal with Le Caron.

Provision also had to be made for rapid reporting if and when the Fenian threat to Canada became more acute. Lord Monck, the Governor-General of Canada, would be ill served if information were first sent to Whitehall and then transmitted back to him in Ottawa.

Thus Le Caron, by arrangement with Anderson, took a trip to Ottawa, where he was received by Judge Gilbert McMicken, the Chief Commissioner of Police.

5

A Suspect Notebook

Detective P. Smith, on his beat in St Armand in February 1868, paused to read a handbill given to him in the street.

EXTRA, GREAT EXCITEMENT!

P. G. Meehan, Editor of the *Irish American* and War Secretary of the Fenian Brotherhood.

Citizens of every creed and from every land, come to Academy Halls this evening, and hear him deliver his great speech on Ireland, commencing 7½ o'clock. Front seats reserved for ladies. Admission free!

GOD SAVE IRELAND

About 1,500 people—a large audience for the locality—responded to the invitation. Three and a half hours later the meeting was still proceeding with no slackening of enthusiasm, but Smith had enough for his report and he went home. His companion stayed behind; he would be one of the young men to enter an adjacent room, which was ostentatiously guarded, as a volunteer for the Fenian Brotherhood—and as a police informer.

Summing up the speeches, the detective wrote: 'They spoke of O'Neill's bravery with his own Irishmen whipping the redcoats at Ridgeway, and how Sweeney [sic] at St Albans disarmed his men when he ought not to, and the time was coming when they would sweep the cursed flag from Canada.'

That report appeared on the desk of Judge Gilbert McMicken, along with papers dealing with all kinds of crime. Counterfeit currency, illicit stills, smuggling, a suspected abortionist, a broken stained-glass window at a Catholic church—all disregard of the law claimed the personal attention of the Chief Commissioner of Police. Sometimes there were warnings of possible trouble: 'A party of six roughs arrived and are hanging about.' At this time he was much occupied with the threat of a Fenian attack across the border and a possible revolt of the Irish in Canada, and he wrote frequent appreciations of the situation for the Prime Minister, Sir John Macdonald.

Ample confirmation of the excitement engendered at meetings came from several quarters. An agent had attended a crowded one in Buffalo addressed by General O'Neill and had concluded that 'there will be work for us all before long'.

With warnings of this kind coming in, it is no wonder that Judge McMicken wrote on 24 February 1868 in these terms:

> I am fully persuaded that an attempt at invasion will be made this spring or early in the summer and that it will be made with all the desperate energy they can call forth. It behoves timely preparation to be made for it, although I do not think it at all necessary for some time yet to call out any of the volunteer force or incur any great expense. I have every confidence in being well informed about the actual movement when about to take place.

He was now actively recruiting agents on both sides of the border. In March he appointed 'four good men' in Guelph (Ontario) 'for the discovery of leading Fenians in that neighbourhood and for keeping a constant watch upon their doings'. In pursuit of this operation he asked permission to inspect letters passing through the Guelph post office. A few weeks later several local Fenians were arrested.

Across the border, in Malone, where they had no powers of arrest, members of his force were watching the surreptitious unloading of arms.

The network operated well, but it was producing mostly low-level intelligence. McMicken must at times have sighed wearily as he turned over his informants' offerings, trying to decide what they all amounted to. Some of the correspondents were semi-literate; they habitually wrote 'I would of' and such phonetic versions of everyday speech and they were inclined to use several octave sheets before coming to the point. Such men were not to be judged as detectives by their syntax and spelling; they could move usefully among the suspect roughs and discover what was going on, but their observations were necessarily confined to their own class. Other informants wrote in the copperplate hand then essential to clerks; their letters were less trying to read and contained information from well-informed citizens such as doctors and bank managers and from members of Fenian circles—some were officials of circles. There were the police constables, using the prescribed form ('I have the honour to report . . .'), meticulous at following suspects, giving a detailed account of how they had spent their duty hours. McMicken could justly claim a regular flow of information, but sentiment on the ground, constantly stirred up by marches, demonstrations, manifestos and urgent appeals for funds, was no reliable guide to what was going on at the top.

In June 1868 that situation changed with the arrival of a sizeable packet of documents containing all the current information available at the Fenian Brotherhood headquarters. Le Caron had filled the gap.

This first communication seemed to confirm the predictions of an imminent invasion. It included an instruction to organizers by O'Neill, dated 13 June, to ban after 15 June all public meetings, balls, picnics and announcements of the arrival and departure of officers. When this order was conveyed to the circles it produced, as McMicken noted, 'considerable excitement and ardour among the Brotherhood'. The accounts, however, as copied by Le Caron, cast doubt on the Brotherhood's ability to finance an attack. The balance in the organization's treasury was only $9,967.98, after 600 circles, with 3,600 collectors, had in May raised income totalling $6,658.65.

Le Caron's despatch contained one of O'Neill's long statements. After congratulating the officers and men of the Brotherhood 'on the continued progress of the organization—on the advance of the national column on the road that leads to the liberation of Ireland' he repeated a claim that the Brotherhood Senate constituted the only existing elected Irish Government and that it proved the capacity of the Irish people for self-government. He proceeded:

> Although not recognized as a Power among the nations we have made ourselves felt as such. We have to a great extent controlled the destinies of the British Empire and compelled the Ministers of that tyrannical Government to shape their measures and abandon their traditional policy in order to *evade* the difficulties in which we

place them, and which they confess themselves still unable to overcome . . . . Brothers, do not mistake our purpose or our policy. We have learnt wisdom in the hard school of experience and we do not lightly sacrifice the advantages of our present position or risk the national cause on a rash venture.

Several passages indicated the continuing split in the Irish movement and claimed that only his section represented the will of the people. Critics who doubted the military capability to undertake another operation were assured: 'Some of the first military men of America have already offered their services.'

The military instructions enclosed laid down that regiments should consist of ten companies; that the flanking companies should be armed with breech loaders and the others with muzzle loaders; that only unmarried men should be recruited for the campaign; that no business men should be enlisted if they were likely to use their business commitments as an excuse for not promptly obeying orders; and that enlistment should be confined as far as possible to large places from which men could be moved without creating suspicion.

An appeal for funds asserted that the Irish in America sent home $4 million annually which went into the pockets of the Irish land-lords 'and one half of which, if applied to the rescue of their native land, would restore liberty and prosperity to the Irish people at home and relieve their friends here from a permanent tax to which there now appears to be no end'.

The documents bore the warning: 'Look out for Spies.'

'My chief informant now occupies an excellent position and writes me daily,' wrote Judge McMicken to Sir John Macdonald. The regular information from Le Caron enabled the Canadian authorities to keep their fingers constantly on the Fenian pulse. In July 1868 the Judge could report that the danger of attack had receded, that the higher ranks were grumbling and discontented because money was not coming in. The Senate of the Brotherhood issued what were to become periodic statements counselling patience, exhorting members to keep their long-term aims in mind, warning them to be discreet. At times it seemed that attack was near. O'Neill, apparently engaged in detailed planning, asked Le Caron to take a cavalry command of 150 men. When the time came, several units of this kind would make their way into Canada, seize horses and 'by a system of rapid marches and depredations strike terror into the people'.

In September McMicken summarized the reports: 'They appear just now to be at their wits' end.' To raise morale O'Neill, in October, promised an early statement to show that 'Your officers have already made arrangements with men who have at once the will and the ability to serve Ireland not in conventions or in diplomatic discussions—but on the field of battle where the only arguments that will carry weight will be the bullets and cold steel of Irish soldiers.' But in that month the reason for postponing a move was that negotiations were proceeding for an alliance between the leading generals of the late Confederacy of the Southern States. At a secret meeting in New York in July eight of the southern generals had been present, and they had agreed to bring all the men and resources in their power to take Canada from the British, 'the Fenians to use said country as a base for operations against Great Britain and then to give over Canada to said Southerners for their services rendered'.

Having learned that the Fenian Brotherhood was already bargaining away Canada, McMicken, unperturbed but watchful, awaited details of how the first part of the plan was to be put into effect. Then Le Caron ran into trouble.

As the Brotherhood's scheme for a successful invasion depended partly on a simultaneous uprising of Irish sympathizers in Canada, the Judge wanted to know the identity of potential leaders in his territory. With this in mind, Le Caron approached a man named John Roche, who had originally lived in Montreal. They met at a secret council, held in Troy House, Troy, New York, in November 1868, to discuss the next invasion. Le Caron told Roche that he had been ordered by O'Neill to visit enemy territory and contact a few reliable 'brothers' there. Roche gave him several names, which Le Caron immediately entered in a notebook. Something about his inquirer's manner, possibly the alacrity with which he had written down the names, caused Roche to have misgivings. He took to observing Le Caron, and as he did so his suspicions grew. He decided to act quickly.

That same month, at the Annual Convention in the Masonic Hall, Philadelphia, he formally charged Le Caron with carelessness, dangerous conduct and suspicious acts.

6

A Delicate Situation

Six thousand armed and uniformed Fenians paraded raggedly through the streets of Philadelphia, behind the flag which had been carried at Ridgeway, to mark the Fenian Brotherhood Convention of 1868. Four hundred delegates assembled, in an atmosphere of smoke and tavern fumes, jostling each other and shouting.

Besides Le Caron, attending as the delegate from Illinois, several agents covered the proceedings for McMicken. One of their tasks was to identify the Canadian representatives, of whom three or four were known to be present, but tough Fenians kept them too well guarded for the detectives from over the border to approach them.

The Convention's purpose was to demonstrate militancy, to whip up enthusiasm, to rake in funds while the emotion was at its height, but at the same time to fend off the wilder spirits who were eager to march on the frontier at an hour's notice. Militancy and enthusiasm were readily aroused; cash came less easily. 'The Irish race throughout the world' was appealed to for money and, specifically, every Irish man and woman in the United States—a familiar fund-raising trick in all movements—was asked to send one dollar; in theory it is a simple way to raise millions, but in practice it never works. Pending this avalanche of dollars, a subscription list was circulated; the signatories merely made promises without actually having to put their hands in their pockets. Following the signature of P. O'Day was the handsome figure of $500; the subscriber, perhaps having in mind the free-spending reputation of some of the leaders, stipulated that the sum should be spent on converting 100 muzzle loaders to breech loaders. O'Neill put his name down for $100. Le Caron, discreetly not vying with his leader but showing an acceptable generosity, signed for $60.

A committee which investigated why a military move had not yet been made was cynical about promises of subscriptions. At the Cleveland Convention, it pointed out, $167,450 had been pledged, but of this sum $112,363, more than two-thirds, had not yet been paid. A hint was dropped of another possible source of funds—'in the favourable circumstances of a national election, a large amount of money could be procured from American politicians.'

Delegates with their wits about them would have read into the proceedings several indications that there was to be no immediate call to arms. Those who had supposed that there should be were reproached:

> Your Committee see in the action of your President and Senate, in refusing to make a movement without the preparation and means required to promise success, the triumph of moral heroism, of conscience and judgment over the recklessness and passion of impatience; and discover in it that prudence, that foresight and firmness, which is the highest testament of their past conduct, and the best guarantee of the future safety and success of the movement in their hands.

This eloquent self-approbation was made plausible by comparisons with the rash behaviour of Fenians in Ireland and England in the previous year. Ill-prepared risings in Ireland were easily suppressed; agents who had infiltrated a gang planning to raid the arms store at Chester Castle in England ruined the scheme. Back from a visit to Ireland, the Brotherhood's Secretary of Civil Affairs, Daniel O'Sullivan, uttered some harsh criticisms. The organization over there, he reported, was practically powerless and disbanded, its leaders had 'rushed into the field the noble, brave and generous fellows who composed it'. He condemned as too costly the rescue from the prison van in Manchester: 'Kelly and Deasey were set free, it is true; but therefore three men, better, purer and braver ascended the scaffold; many others pined for months in prison, and some are still pining.' After deploring the aftermath of the Clerkenwell explosion, O'Sullivan concluded that the Irish at home could achieve nothing without American help.

O'Neill, a skilled morale-raiser, was now able to present himself as a prudent planner whose aggression was nevertheless undiminished. Responding to his speech, the conference confirmed the plan for a second invasion of Canada, without committing the Senate to when it should take place.

To give verisimilitude to the claim that the headquarters in New York constituted a legitimate government, a printed report of the Convention was issued in the form of a typical government document. The title in Gothic type read: 'Proceedings of the Senate and House of Representatives of the Fenian Brotherhood'.

The leadership could congratulate itself on handling the conference well but, awaiting the outcome of the investigation, Le Caron was anxious. Although he appeared self-possessed as he viewed the scene from behind a cigar, and his brain responded effectively in awkward situations, he was by nature excitable, impulsive and nervous. So far protected by O'Neill, who gave him his complete trust, to others he seemed an outsider. He tried to avert suspicion by always taking a conventional line and invariably siding with the majority, yet now, through Roche's accusations, he was exposed to investigation. The Irish, and with good reason, were obsessed with treachery, and prone to attribute every setback to betrayal. It needed just one careless move on his part and the whole pack would be after him.

Fortunately the investigating committee confined themselves to the one issue of the entries in his notebook. On this matter he was, as civil servants say, 'covered'. He rebutted Roche's charges by producing a letter dated 23 October 1868, from the Brotherhood's headquarters, signed by the President, authorizing him to avail himself 'of every opportunity to study the country on both sides of the line for future emergencies'. The committee reported in favour of Le Caron.

Now he saw the chance to consolidate his position by adopting a pose of injured innocence. In hurt tones he wrote to headquarters to the effect that, because his trustworthiness had been impugned, he wished to resign as an officer of the Irish Republican Army. This gamble could have failed if someone sufficiently influential at headquarters judged that, although Le Caron's motives were not in question, he was dangerously careless in keeping secret information in a notebook which might be mislaid or stolen. But he had correctly anticipated the reaction from New York. The War Department replied assuring him that the President wanted him to remain an officer of the organization. The writer, J. Whitehead Byron, Colonel and Acting Adjutant-General, added:

> Your services have been thoroughly appreciated both by him and the officials of both Departments, civil and military, therefore you should not notice the innuendoes or taunts of parties who cannot value your services. If the officers of the organization who have been vilified and calumniated were to resign on that account, some of its best officers would not now be at their post. The 'Patriot's meed is bitter'; they must bear with much, even from those who should be the first to defend and sustain them.

Le Caron withdrew his resignation but he gave up keeping a notebook. It was a wise decision for a man who wanted to get people talking. Every experienced interviewer must have noticed that someone who is chatting freely will freeze up as soon as he starts to take notes. The talker sees that the situation has now changed; instead of just gossiping he is making a statement; remarks are being turned into what may become a permanent record, available to all who have access to it. Roche had taught Le Caron a valuable lesson.

Another potential danger area lay in Canadian government offices. Although McMicken wrote his letters himself, his lengthy correspondence with the Prime Minister about Le Caron must at some point have been handled by clerks. McMicken's statements of 'special disbursements', as the payments to secret agents were termed, disclosed his full name and the amounts paid to him; in the first nine months of 1869 he and two others, named as J. M. McDonald and W. Montgomery (cover name McMichael), all received the same pay of $76 a month. An unexplained payment by cheque of $100 to Le Caron's wife was made in January; she acknowledged it to 'Jas. Bell, Esq.' in Ottawa, signing herself 'Mrs Nannie Le Caron'. Frequent telegrams not in code, sent through the Montreal Telegraph Company, referred to 'LeC'; not until later was he sometimes called Beach or by an invented name. McMicken travelled to Chicago and had long talks with Le Caron. Did the Fenians never trail the Canadian Chief Commissioner of Police? Had they no contacts among hotel receptionists and porters? Everybody was apparently as incurious as the postal staff in Nashville.

As an agent he possessed a strange immunity. Nothing disturbed the supply of information to Ottawa. McMicken analysed the Brotherhood's monthly accounts with the keenness of an auditor. 'The leaders have not forgotten the interests of "Number One",' he commented in May 1869, after comparing the organization's costs for the previous months. Expenses had risen although the number of paid organizers had fallen. He queried an item of $7,519.56 for the 'alteration of arms', observing 'apparently a very convenient cover for the abstraction of funds'. He speculated whether O'Neill and Meehan, seeing that supporters were disheartened, 'might get up a show for what appears to me their recent plunder of the funds'.

Away from headquarters it certainly looked as though the show was not far off. At Trenton, New Jersey, a small factory supervised by a master armourer was converting muzzle loaders to breech loaders capable of firing twenty shots a minute. A large quantity of new green clothing was unloaded at the organization's stores in Clifton, and the Ogdensburg branch received a heavy box containing army belts. Arms were being secretly stored at several places along the frontier; often they were hidden in packages labelled as groceries or hardware under well-known importers' names and sent to business addresses. Food was deposited along the New York and Vermont frontiers; Le Caron supplied a complete list of the provisions in stock and sent McMicken some biscuits which had been warehoused for two years. McMicken tasted them and, forwarding a sample to the Prime Minister, remarked that the quality was unimpaired. Fenian groups were drilling regularly and openly parading. Concealed among onlookers McMicken watched a procession in July at Windsor and observed with satisfaction that his agent McDonald, marching at the head of a company, was the most soldierly of the lot: 'A fine-looking man—half the others raw recruits, 120 military in a procession of 400.'

Every rise and fall in spirits at Fenian headquarters was registered in Ottawa. In June 1869 a serious dispute broke out because several Fenian officers, anxious to fight somebody if the Canadians were not to be immediately tackled, proposed an expedition to help the Cubans throw off Spanish domination. Reports circulated that Fenian arms stored at Buffalo in preparation for the attack on Canada were being diverted to Cuba; to allay unrest among their followers headquarters issued a denial that any war material was sold to the Cubans. To onlookers it seemed that O'Neill's hand would be forced and that a raid must be attempted that summer. But one fact enabled the Canadian authorities to sit back and allow their volunteer reservists to continue in their civilian occupations. O'Neill wanted Le Caron by his side before the action began. It had been agreed that O'Neill would not ask him to leave his home and his medical practice until everything was nearly ready. Although active in the movement, Le Caron had not yet received the summons.

Expectations were raised when, in August, the Senate made an urgent appeal to circles for $5,000, concluding: 'It will be the last time you will be called upon, except to *transport your fighting men in face of the enemy*.' Agents picked up the reaction in the local circles; the captain at a Fenian rally in Buffalo told one of them that they would invade Canada before the end of the month. Nothing further came from headquarters until September; then O'Neill sent out a printed appeal for every man to contribute $10 to a Special War Fund. Leading executive members argued that funds were still insufficient for an operation and one of the Brotherhood Senate wrote to O'Neill: 'It is a sacrifice of noble men's lives and therefore it is a crime to move this winter.' Tempers, never very even, were being strained. McMicken's agent Montgomery, a member of a Fenian circle in New York, wrote in October that during a drill session a serious fight broke out between two officers and 'while endeavouring to make peace I got badly hurt'. In his summing-up of the overall situation the Judge wrote to Sir John: 'They seem passing through the phase of the Kilkenny cat operation from which I hope we may soon hear of them emerging in like condition to their prototypes of the story.'

In a later communication, McMicken warned the Prime Minister that, despite the unfavourable state of the organization, the Irish temperament had to be taken into account: 'With any other people than the Irish the organization would have ceased to exist ere now and whatever weaknesses appear in it at present is no criterion of future action—many things indicate the impossibility of a move now—such as the recent falling away of attendances at circle meetings, the very many non-paying members.'

So confident was McMicken that his penetration of the target organization was adequate that he now rejected approaches by would-be informers. The Prime Minister's office forwarded to him an offer from a Fenian officer in Chicago. McMicken returned it with a covering letter addressed to Sir John: 'Be assured that nothing of importance in regard to a Fenian movement can take place in

Chicago without my being apprised of it. Chicago, Buffalo and New York I have at present under good and reliable supervision.—Le Caron is in the neighbourhood of Chicago and he is always informed when any active effort of movement is on foot.' When another Fenian circle secretary offered headquarters documents McMicken explained to the Prime Minister that these would be too stale. Tactful replies were drafted to these and other Brotherhood members.

Unless such potential informers were penetration agents, briefed by the Brotherhood, it is difficult to understand how they could, with such insouciance, write to a government office where they had no friendly contacts, giving their names, addresses and positions in a revolutionary movement, and offer to break their oaths and betray their associates. There is no way of knowing whether some of them were exposed and silenced, but this could not have happened sufficiently often to be a deterrent. As it was, they entrusted their safety to the discretion of civil servants.

By October it seemed certain that the year would pass without an attack on Canada. While on a tour, visiting his agents, McMicken wired Sir John: 'Gold looking doubtful for speedy issue.' Le Caron, however, argued that, with the Ninth Annual Convention of the Brotherhood due in December, O'Neill must 'create some sensational stir such as the Ridgeway affair' if he wanted to keep his post as president. At a meeting with the Judge in Windsor he voiced fears about his personal safety. He could not back out now, he said, but must stick by O'Neill and he trusted that everything possible would be done to secure him from harm. He pointed out that he had a wife and two children and a medical practice which brought him from $10 to $12 a day. Also, he added, he had just paid the fee for a course of lectures which, if away for any time, he would be unable to attend. McMicken added a postscript to a letter to the Prime Minister: 'LeC is really in a delicate position and feels anxious about his information not being used in any way to bring him under suspicion—I need not urge these considerations upon you but in duty to him I mention it.'

In a personal letter to Le Caron O'Neill appointed him Lieutenant-Colonel and Acting Adjutant-General of the Irish Republican Army at a salary of $100 a month and asked him to report to New York early in November. The letter was signed: 'Your friend.'

7

To Fulfil the Contract

If any confirmation had been needed of O'Neill's confidence in Le Caron, it would have been provided by an incident during the Ninth Annual Convention of the Fenian Brotherhood in New York City in December 1869. O'Neill confessed to him that he had been drawing on the organization's funds for his personal needs. Professor Brophy (described by Le Caron as 'one of the few honest deluded patriots of the time') was refusing as treasurer to cook the accounts for presentation to the Convention, and O'Neill wanted to borrow $364.41 urgently. Le Caron lent him the money, and later received a receipt dated 19 April 1870.

A council of war, meeting during the Convention, decided to start the operation against Canada in the spring, as soon as the condition of the roads permitted military movements. Summarized, the plan was to attack Canada from three points, Buffalo, Malone and Franklin, and to seize enough territory to form a base for operations against the British forces. In the first forays the movement of the Canadian defenders was to be hampered by cutting railways and destroying canal systems, while the following Fenian troops dug themselves in and awaited reinforcements. Ports and dockyards would be seized, from which English shipping could be attacked. Once a substantial position was consolidated, the invaders could claim belligerent rights from the United States. This concession would permit large reinforcements of veterans from both sides in the civil war to cross the border; experienced officers, it was asserted, had already promised their support. No attempt was to be made to establish an Irish republic on Canadian soil.

The British Government in London, faced with this occupation of part of its empire, was to be forced to negotiate the independence of Ireland.

Colonel Clingen was put in charge of arms distribution for the west and Le Caron for the east sector. In the office to which O'Neill had appointed him Le Caron was the only person who knew the position of all the secret stores. On extensive tours he checked the locations of every depot and sent McMicken in letters and cipher telegrams the precise figures available of muzzle loaders, breech loaders, rounds of ammunition, uniforms (among them seventy-five British uniforms brought in by deserters), greatcoats, belts, blankets, barrels of pork and of hard bread. Within a month of compiling these extensive lists he had to revise them because a meeting at headquarters, after 'a long confab', decided to shift the material as near the border as possible. He felt that to move everything was too big a job, but he organized parties which, sworn to secrecy and working at night, moved substantial quantities of material. At this stage of his work he made up his mind that it was time to carry a pistol.

This small, lean man had remarkable stamina. Where the rail did not run he travelled by stage, or he hired a buggy or a saddle horse and made his way over unmade, rutted roads. While staying in sparsely furnished, cold and ill-lit hotels he wrote to McMicken in Ottawa and Anderson in London at a length which must sometimes have robbed him of hours of sleep. He never mentioned feeling tired yet his handwriting, bold at the start of a letter, after several pages became struggling, he neglected punctuation and he made slips of the pen. He worried about his wife and children. Asking McMicken for a pass on the Grand Trunk Railway in January 1870, so that he could go home for a few days, he acknowledged a cheque sent to his wife: '. . . am very glad, thank you, for she would have been awful hard up without me—I've plenty owing me if I could be there and look after it. She says she will be all right to the 1st of Feb—you will not forget her please. I am getting a head in cash this month but I don't know if I can raise enough to buy a coat which I want awful guess O'N and Keenan [the Fenian Secretary for Civil Affairs] will never pay me. . . . Awful job to stay away from home. . . . They think it awfully cruel of me if twer not for your kindness I would have to throw up the sponge but I'll stick.' He knew, he added, that the United States authorities, acting on information supplied by the Canadian Government, were on their

From 30-8-55

Burlington Feb 24/70

Y. McMicken Esqr
    Dear Sir

Enclosed Circulars will show you at once why O'N is hurrying me up. I am full of business. 48 cases of material arrived since I was here last & I have now 18 cases more. 80,000 rounds of B. Loading Ammunition from N.Y. & more Carbines. B. Loaders, & 11 cases of them ordered to night — I have number of letters. I require them to answer, & refer to them — I shall be in Ogdensburgh — at Seymour House on Sunday next — getting there Saturday night & I shall leave there monday night — will you have someone there to hand me back these circulars & 8 letters as I require them — I would rather see you than anyone — & can show you the rest you see I may not be near you again for I go to N.Y. shortly — 10th of March just think — 2 weeks now —

                Thigin Thu
                R. G. Syer —

I have given Dr. Pass — $15.00

(left margin:) Ans & tell him I will come to your town — Monday will do if more convenient to you

Using a cover name, Le Caron reports to his spymaster, McMicken.
'Thigin Thu' is Irish for 'Do you understand?'

track; United States detectives, under General Sherman's orders, had reported arms at two points along the border, but the General would not seize the arms yet.

This letter was addressed to 'Jas. Bell, Esq.', but it was signed with Le Caron's recently adopted cover name, R.G. Sayer. He was moving about rapidly now, and his projected itinerary was subject to alteration at short notice because of O'Neill's summonses. McMicken's messengers, sent to collect his reports or return circulars and documents, sometimes missed him. Two of McMicken's sons, Alex and Hamilton, both in the police force, were detailed to keep in touch with him. Hamilton went to meet him at Burlington in February but Le Caron failed to arrive. On another occasion, also in Burlington, Le Caron did not recognize McMicken's man, Police Constable Walter Page, who could not publicly approach him. They encountered one another in the hotel entrance but, beyond a glance, Le Caron took no notice of Page. Page waited until 11 o'clock that night, periodically checking that the key to Le Caron's room was hanging in the office. He got up at six o'clock the following morning and saw from the register that Le Caron (whom in his report he called Mr Le C) had already left.

To solve this problem, Le Caron suggested that he should have someone permanently with him. The Judge, after meeting him, agreed and reported to the Prime Minister that he had sent Beach 'one of my outpost force—a respectable and reliable man. He will remain constantly within his reach in order to receive communications as he would not have time otherwise to make.'

This arrangement had an unforeseen consequence. A Fenian sympathizer from Ottawa recognized the respectable and reliable John C. Rose while he was in Malone, N.Y., and denounced him as a Canadian police agent to the local head centre, whose name was G. J. Mannix. Detailed by Mannix, Brotherhood members followed Rose from place to place and observed that he stayed in the same hotels as Le Caron. Rose was careful never to be seen in Le Caron's presence or to give any sign of recognition; how documents were passed from one to the other they never perceived and they entertained no suspicion that the two men were working together. It was obvious to them that Rose was spying on Le Caron. Rose was returning from a post office where he had just sent off one of Le Caron's despatches when they waylaid him and beat him up so badly that he was an invalid for months. Had they made their attack before he had rid himself of the letter, Le Caron's career might have been painfully terminated. As it was, Le Caron had to compliment the attackers on their action.

O'Neill and Le Caron were now frequently travelling together, staying at hotels under assumed names. They must have seemed an odd pair, O'Neill an expansive character who drank heavily, Le Caron reserved and never drinking alcohol. While observing the movement of arms, the Montreal police—unaware of the operations of McMicken's secret branch—had identified the Fenian General and his adjutant. They sent Ottawa a report dated 1 April on the stores which were being shifted about and they added:

> The superintendance of this Branch of the business seems to have devolved upon Colonel Henry Le Caron, whose travelling name is G. R. Smith and is so registered at the Hotels.
>
> Genl. O'Niel is generally attended by him and they have in sleighs been on a tour of inspection they were at Burlington on the 19th and the General registered his name as McClelland and from there to Ogdensburgh &c.

The police reported, correctly, that the plan was to get a foothold on Canadian soil and then await reinforcements, and they had learned the date which was at that time in O'Neill's mind. They concluded:

> Everything is being done very quietly—nothing apparent on the surface.
>
> Friday April 13 is the day named for the raid. . . . The roads are in such a state that it will be almost an impossibility to move any quantity of stores or persons by that time. If they cut the telegraph almost the same difficulties will prevent the Canadian Government from sending or massing troops to repel them.

The Montreal police, although McMicken had very properly concealed from them Le Caron's true function, had a good source. They reported a Fenian plan to send an officer and twenty-five or thirty mounted men ahead, each with a spare bridle, to stop residents driving off their cattle and horses. This information had originally been passed to the British Consul in New York, Edwin Mortimer Archibald, by his own paid informer inside the Fenian headquarters, Major Rudolph Fitzpatrick, who held the office of Assistant Secretary of War. It was Major Fitzpatrick who had been entrusted with the organization and leadership of this raiding party. Amused by the appointment, McMicken noted: '. . . it is not likely he will place any serious obstacle in the way of the farmers moving their horses.' Some time later the Montreal police obtained details of a similar raiding party to be led by one of their informants, a head centre; he provided what appeared to be sound information about the disposition of the attacking forces, and the Montreal commissioner was so impressed that he proposed to keep two men in constant contact with him and to organize a mounted relay to forward his despatches.

Events had now gone so far that the Fenian Brotherhood was faced with either an early attack or a shameful withdrawal. Dissension showed itself in several alterations in the date of the next Congress. Financial troubles increased. The arms factory machinery at Trenton, which had cost $40,000, was put up for sale; the best offer for it was only $8,000. It had already converted enough Springfield rifles for the attacking force's needs but at an inflated cost; whereas the Colts Arms Manufacturing Company had tendered to undertake the conversion at $6.50 a rifle, the outlay in the Trenton factory was calculated to have been $13.50 a rifle. Having no taxpayers to alleviate its managerial disasters, the Irish Government in exile could only call for more and more subscriptions. At the beginning of April the Long Island Circle alone raised $800, some of the members borrowing the money for their contributions. McMicken's New York agent, McMichael, himself donated $25. The circle was under the impression that its fighting men (whose travelling expenses it would have to pay) would be called up within a few days. Some of the Fenian force were already moving northwards. On 8 April Walter Page reported from Hamilton, N.Y., that 'a considerable number of hard cases have arrived here within the last few days principally by trains from the east and are loafing about the city with no apparent object. They are men of the Fenian stamp and are gathering here for no good purpose.' Other reports mentioned the mood among Irish dock labourers and threats of sabotage to the Welland Canal.

In Vermont a member of the state legislature was asked by a group of men for permission to store cases in an empty barn he owned. Innocently he consented but later, hearing rumours of clandestine activities, he became curious and opened a case. Hurriedly he requested a friend, General George P. Foster, the

United States Marshal for the Northern District of Vermont, to call. The ammunition Foster saw in the barn was tangible confirmation of many reports he had received. He journeyed to Montreal to call on the Commissioner of Police, to whom he explained that if he were ordered to make seizures he had no military force to support the civil power if resistance were offered. Another danger existed which the Commissioner summarized in a memorandum: 'The Militia in the State of Vermont had been for some time past steadily filled up by Irishmen and if the Government called them out to support the civil power or to prevent the passage of men across the Border that both officers and men with U.S. arms in their hands would join the Fenians, and it had even been said it was part of the programme.' General Foster added that it would be at least ten to twelve days before General Grant could get troops to the state.

'*Must see you*,' wrote Le Caron from Troy, using the name of Sayer. 'Brady [the code name for O'Neill] will fill the contract on his own responsibility on the 15th day of April.'

On 11 April the Canadian Government ordered general mobilization. Sir George E. Cartier, the Minister of Militia and Defence, gave orders to cover the entire frontier as occasion required. Five thousand men guarded the frontier of the province of Quebec, where the main attack was anticipated. Mobile reserves were held at Montreal and Quebec. Companies of the Grand Trunk Railway Brigade were posted at vulnerable sections of the system. All troops were at their posts within forty-eight hours. To the Government it was a very satisfactory exercise. Knowing that it had adequate forces to meet an emergency, the Government released the troops from duty between 21 and 29 April.

The demonstration shocked the Fenian leaders. Characteristically, O'Neill responded by getting drunk. As far back as 11 February he had signed a directive—not apparently sent out until some weeks later—putting his forces on the alert. Expressions of impatience had been reaching New York from the local centres for a long time. O'Neill was even drunk when he faced a full attendance of officers at headquarters. There was no doubt, he roared, that a traitor was among them. To those who were discouraged by the Canadians' activities on the frontier, he said they should not be disheartened by a few days' delay. After an excited discussion the officers decided to postpone the invasion but to no distant date.

Commenting on O'Neill's behaviour, McMicken's agent,

McMichael, speculated on whether the General might have been play-acting 'as he is a cunning fox'. However, he did not doubt that 'the preparations made by the Canadians have almost scared the life out of him but if he does not fight he must leave the organization in disgrace'. Strangely, considering the purpose of the meeting, a priest from Ireland was present. He was visiting the United States to collect funds for a church in Armagh. O'Neill's condition raised no question in his mind as to its cause; he simply thought that the General had had too much to drink, and afterwards (according to McMichael) 'he told us that he believed now what he never did before that there is a curse on the Fenians'.

O'Neill's addiction did not affect his standing with the Brotherhood, who were not men to be shocked by anyone with a taste for whisky. The Congress in April re-elected him president, and reaffirmed its faith in W. Egan, the vice-president, and the council of eight, who were described by McMicken as 'all of the same stamp of mind, reckless and rude, fitting coadjutors of O'Neill'. The military department, however, was still pleading for delay on the grounds that although it held 23,000 stands of arms of all kinds, it calculated that another 500,000 rounds of ammunition were needed.

Le Caron was present, with Constable Page in attendance to forward his reports. The crowd and the general bustle at the Congress made letter-writing impossible, so he scribbled rough notes. This time he was able to give McMicken the name of a delegate from Montreal, but he expressed the standing fear of agents that their information will be used in a way which compromises them. He appealed for this man, Rapple, to be left alone. Fenian contacts in Canada were obviously trying to discover the source of leaks from New York. One, a Father Griffiths, whose locality was unknown, knew someone 'having something to do with the Government' and from this official the priest had learned that a member of the Brotherhood staff was in constant communication with the Canadian Government. If a civil servant in Ottawa knew that much, he was presumably on the look-out for that little more which would enable him to identify the traitors.

Apart from providing Le Caron with the discreet PC Page to get his reports away quickly and unobtrusively, McMicken did what he could for the safety of Le Caron and the other agents. Telegrams were now sent in cipher; it was a simple system based on a displacement of the letters of the alphabet (the recipient only needed to know which letter stood for 'A') and any code-breaker could have cracked it easily, but a curious telegraphist, working at speed, would have made nothing of it. Telegrams in clear were made to look like business messages; 'cheese' meant arms and to 'fulfil the contract' referred to the start of hostilities. Le Caron was no longer 'LeC' or 'Beach' but always 'Sayer'. As the Fenians knew McMichael by his real name of William Montgomery, his customary cover name was retained.

McMicken was also confronted by another problem, of which his agents frequently reminded him. Three or four of them would probably be involved in the attack. He hoped that they would be able to withdraw before the fighting started, but obviously they could not run away in the face of the enemy. If not killed or wounded, they might be taken prisoner and receive some rough treatment, if no worse. Le Caron, in urging the Canadian authorities to crush the invaders so thoroughly that they would never make another attempt, had tentatively mentioned hanging prisoners. McMicken and his men had no illusions about the situation when the forces clashed.

Although it was as complete as could be expected, intelligence coverage of the April Congress was not costly. Le Caron got $91 for the whole month and $45 expenses; Page's salary as a full-time policeman was $45 a month and his duty trip to New York from Ottawa, including his return fare, cost $70.

In the last week of April McMicken received a message which caused him to arrange an early meeting with Le Caron. He wrote to the Prime Minister: 'Beach is getting tired of the work and desires to leave it—or if wanted to continue must have some new arrangement as he cannot support his family without an increase of allowance, etc.'

8

A Tense Wait

'The worst of these fellows is that they only talk of coming instead of actually appearing. If we could only get them to come somewhere in force, I think they would regret it and cease bothering the country.' Lieutenant-Colonel Elphinstone, of Montreal, wrote that in a private letter in April 1870; it echoes what was being said in clubs and wherever military men met. Judge McMicken similarly expressed his feelings to the Prime Minister: 'I most sincerely hope the vagabonds will make their appearance this time and meet their just deserts.'

Rumours kept pace with the mounting excitement on each side of the border. A journalist in Sherbrooke, Quebec Province, overheard Irishmen in a tavern assert confidently that 20,000 men would move on Toronto, followed by another 20,000 who would occupy the city. In Buffalo Brotherhood membership increased daily. Fenians in Malone, N.Y., impatiently waiting to move, grumbled that O'Neill lacked energy and showed no evidence of leadership. They did not know that back in New York the General was having trouble with the Senate, where James Gibbons, the President, still thought an attack premature.

O'Neill was determined to justify his undertakings. He ensured that his mobilization order was now in the hands of all units. It stipulated that uniforms and insignia were not to be worn *en route* and officers must not be recognized by military titles. Officers were to take no man who had not seen service, who would not be of good behaviour on the journey and in the presence of the enemy. There followed an injunction which, in the event, was not strictly obeyed:

58

'Take no man who is a loafer or an habitual drunkard.' Arms were to be forwarded to designated points. 'Let no consideration of business prevent a prompt compliance with this order,' O'Neill concluded.

In the second week of May he summoned his commanders, rather to their surprise as they had expected a longer delay. Le Caron had received no firm information to the effect that a move was imminent, and on getting a wire to report to O'Neill he hastily telegraphed the authorities in Ottawa to arrange to meet Canadian agents in Buffalo. On joining O'Neill in that town, he was appointed Adjutant-General with the rank of Brigadier-General. He comments: 'We had quick promotion and brave ranks in the Fenian army!'

Police Constable James Schryer, one of McMicken's men who had crossed from Fort Erie, and who numbered a doctor and a gunsmith among his contacts in Buffalo, promptly reported that O'Neill was staying at a hotel called the Mansion House.

From inside the Mansion House McMicken was receiving a lot of information. Earlier in the month he had seen the somewhat dispirited Le Caron and spoken to him about money. It is unlikely that his principal agent could have pulled out at that stage anyway, and the suspicion must arise that Le Caron was forcing the issue of payment at the time when his services were most needed; but what he really wanted was probably recognition. His position was lonely and he constantly reached out to people who could share his secret and appreciate the importance of his work. In doing so he ran risks which sometimes alarmed McMicken. Whatever the truth, the Judge talked him out of his mood, and the result of Le Caron's reporting was embodied in a memorandum dated 22 May addressed to Sir George E. Cartier, the Minister of Militia and Defence. The attack would be made, McMicken wrote, 'on Wednesday or Thursday night 25/26 inst.' The memorandum gave detailed planned movements of contingents, the two points of attack, and where feints were to be made 'by way of boasting noise, etc.' It was believed that the Fenians would be unable to mass any large number of men, and they had no money. O'Neill had had a serious quarrel with Egan, the vice-president of the organization and the best man of his new council. Colonel Lewis of Vermont had been accused of treachery in informing the Canadian Government of the intended movement. 'They lose in him the strongest individual they have. . . .' McMicken enclosed photographs of O'Neill and Colonels Lewis and Clingen.

(The information that O'Neill had lost Lewis's services was false. Accusations were hastily made and quickly forgotten. Lewis remained on the staff.)

Fenian movements were well monitored by government agencies and newspapers. Railroad offices at important western points stayed open all night, and records were kept of the numbers travelling. Passengers who happened to be on the same trains as the Fenians said that they mostly seemed to be in a genial mood, circulating whisky bottles and occasionally roaring 'The Wearin' o' the Green'. One travel agent was asked to quote an excursion fare for 2,000 men but declined. Heavy traffic by road was also noted. Eighty-five loaded teams passed through Fairield, Maine; the hired teamsters, as part of their contract, had been promised a share of the loot. All drinking places were closed there, and Fenians were buying food at the local shops and from farmers. About 100 boxes were unloaded at Cook's Corners; they looked like ordinary commercial crates as the rifles they contained had been taken to pieces. Large numbers of saddles, to equip stolen horses, were observed near the frontier. St Albans, Vermont, was a main assembly point, and an estimated 2,000 Fenians had already arrived there. The United States Marshal reported to the Canadian military headquarters in Montreal on the troop and freight movements and commented: 'My instructions are merely to report movements. If required to stop them will require troops.'

During the night of 23–4 May the Montreal Telegraph Company's cable crossing the St Lawrence River from Prescott to Ogdensburg was cut.

It was the eve of the Queen's birthday. The citizens of Montreal knew nothing of the state of alert at the military headquarters there. A Canadian reporter, with a liking for the picturesque phrase, wrote: 'The great city, however, slept in ignorance, and looked forward to as peaceful a Queen's Birthday as had ever sunned its banners.'

Far from being sunned, the banners were drooping. The day, the account continues,

> . . . opened sullenly in Montreal, and the drizzling rain all the forenoon damped the joyful anticipations of many who saw their rare holiday happiness melting away in the watery atmosphere.

Strollers who found their way to the city, perhaps to learn what were the prospects of the review, perhaps for fault of better pastime—for it is singular how many do not know what to do with a holiday—found that rumors were rife in the streets; but they looked with incredulous contempt on the rather general statements of facts which appeared in a newspaper office window, as a holiday *canard* too barefaced to be believed by any one, and an excuse to-day for selling a paper which could conveniently be contradicted on the morrow.

But the day was not without its military spectacle. The review was cancelled, ostensibly because of the weather, but the troops were kept under arms, and by six o'clock that evening five companies, led by two military bands, were marching between cheering crowds to the station. The men were given a typical Victorian send-off. While the train was waiting to start

> . . . there was many a merry leave-taking, chiefly of mere ac-quaintances, here and there of relatives who had accompanied their loved-ones to the train, but in few cases was there any appearance of realizing the undoubtedly serious character of the occasion. . . . From the door and windows of nearly every house which com-manded a view of the train as it passed from the station to the Victoria Bridge, came one continuous cheer and waving of hand-kerchiefs, and the greatest enthusiasm seemed to pervade all classes.

Lieutentant-Colonel W. Osborne Smith, Deputy Adjutant-General of the Fifth Military District of Montreal, appears (accord-ing to one account) to have had a frustrating morning. An author-itative-looking man, with a small beard and waxed moustaches turned up at the ends, he was a born soldier, the son of an officer who had fought at Waterloo and the fourth eldest son in his family to have held a commission in the British army. On receiving intelligence that Fenian soldiers were assembling on the Vermont border he had telegraphed his superiors for instructions, but Ottawa's reply was so tardy that he felt himself justified in invoking the 60th section of the Militia Act which allowed troops to be called out in an emergency. Perhaps O'Neill, in deciding to attack on the Queen's birthday, was thinking not of an affront to the monarch but of the frenzied preparations on which the military mind is concentrated before a parade, when men and horses appear as pretty toys and weapons as glistening ornaments.

Whatever Ottawa's distractions might have been, Colonel Smith had got his men on the move. O'Neill, although so close to the border, was experiencing a much more agonizing delay. He had established himself and his staff at the Franklin Hotel, Franklin, Vermont, and he expected that some 2,000 to 3,000 troops would have assembled in the neighbourhood. Despite all the reports of large numbers of men travelling north, only about 800 presented themselves on 24 May at Hubbard's Farm, the Fenian camp about half a mile away. He sent telegrams and messengers to round up the missing forces, while his officers busied themselves opening cases of arms and distributing rifles and ammunition along the road so that 3,000 men could quickly pick them up. Hours went by and the arms lay there unclaimed.

Any hopes O'Neill might have had of effecting a surprise attack must by now have been dim. That day President Grant issued a proclamation declaring the military movements illegal, and it was obvious that American troops would be advancing in his rear. Pressmen and at least two photographers were hanging about watching everything. 'The scenes in the vicinity of the Fenian headquarters were of a wild and exciting character,' one of them wrote. 'Farmers and tradesmen suspended their labors and anxiously watched, in many cases with great apparent satisfaction, the preparations going forward, and a good many teamsters from the neighbourhood were employed in the transport of the boxes of the Fenians, from various points in the woods in the vicinity.' They were encamped in a dip on high ground opposite Eccles Hill and the plan was to cross from there into Canada, as they had in 1866, and with Eccles Hill as their base to pillage Frelighsburg, Cook's Corners and Pigeon Hill.

In the intense dark of the small hours of 25 May a Fenian captain named Murphy, with a teamster and guide also named Murphy, were making their way through what seemed to be deserted country, searching for the Fenian camp, when they ran into a party of armed men, not in uniform, whom they supposed to be fellow Fenians. The captain showed his commission, signed by O'Neill, and asked the way. They found themselves the prisoners of local Canadian farmers acting as a home guard. After the raid four years earlier, in which their property had suffered, about thirty-five of them, mostly sharp-shooters, had organized themselves for the protection of their farms. Through personal acquaintances on the other side of the frontier they knew of the invasion preparations. They were angry men; the attack was coming in the middle of the sowing season and the interruption could well have cost them a year's crop. They had posted themselves in concealed positions among rocks and brush-wood in front of Eccles Hill, about 300 yards from the boundary.

They handed their prisoners over to a detachment of the 60th Battalion, which had moved up in the dark from Stanbridge. After detailing a corporal and two men to escort the prisoners to Stanbridge, the commander, Lieutenant-Colonel Brown Chamberlin, had a combined force of two officers and seventy-one men. At daybreak they could discern Fenian sentries on a hill on the American side.

9

On to Canada

Behind the brow of the hill opposite the Canadian position, and thus out of sight, the Fenians encamped at Hubbard's Farm moved into the grounds in the rear of a house owned by a Mr Vincent, and there put on their uniforms. A Canadian journalist noted the details: 'The uniform consisted of a dark blue shell-jacket, trimmed with green and yellow braid, pants of dark grey, or in some cases of a light blue colour; nearly all wore the French military cap; their accoutrements were the usual cross and waist-belts, with ammunition pouches and bayonet, while every man was supplied with 40 rounds of ammunition.' The soldiers were, 'for the most part, men about 25 years of age, and the scum of American cities, with a sprinkling of young men who had joined for, as they afterwards expressed it, the fun of making a raid into Canada in the absence of the troops'.

Plenty of people were about in the early morning. On the road running up the valley between the two positions carts jolted along conveying families and household possessions out of the battle area, while sightseers were arriving from St Albans, Highgate, Franklin and the vicinity. The Fenians had put a picket across the road and vehicles approaching the boundary line were being held up. Such conditions enabled Canadian soldiers in civilian clothes to slip across the line, look round and then get back again unnoticed. The confusion favoured Le Caron's messengers, whom he was still keeping busy.

Observing the advanced preparations to flout President Grant's proclamation forbidding a breach of the Neutrality Act, General Foster, in his capacity as United States Marshal, called on O'Neill at the Franklin Hotel, read the proclamation to him, and urged him not to cross the frontier. Suffering as he was from the postponements of the previous day, O'Neill was in no mood even to accord the Marshal a polite hearing. In forcible barrack-room language he expressed his opinion of President Grant, and made it clear that nothing the President or his officers said would deflect the Fenian army from its purpose.

O'Neill did, however, control himself sufficiently to charge his visitor with a message to the Canadian military commander to the effect that his troops would respect women and children, would not plunder peaceable inhabitants, and would conduct the war according to the customs of civilized nations. General Foster had no troops to restrain O'Neill's force, so he left.

At eleven o'clock O'Neill, accompanied by his staff of generals and colonels, emerged from the hotel into the hot sunshine and mounted his horse. Le Caron, one of the high-ranking party, was relishing the fact that after three years of perilous work as an agent of the British and Canadian Governments he was riding close to the General commanding the invasion. Instead of laughing to himself (his own description) he might at this moment have felt a certain pity for a man who regarded him as a close friend and who had reposed such complete trust in him, but he seems to have experienced only amusement, contempt, and satisfaction that he had engineered the downfall of O'Neill and the destruction of the entire enterprise. Having notified McMicken that the attack would definitely come on 25 May, he could face the day with confidence, knowing that the Canadian command must have made its dispositions and that he would not be involved in the fighting. O'Neill's earlier plan that Le Caron would lead a cavalry sweep had long been abandoned. His immediate task was to accompany the General to Hubbard's Farm, await the arrival there of 400 men who were on their way from St Albans, equip them, and see that a field-piece was got into position.

The *Ottawa Citizen* named Le Caron as one of the officers in command of the raid (see Chapter 1), but otherwise he passed unnoticed. A pamphlet produced by Canadian journalists incorporating their reports fails to mention him although it records the names of others on O'Neill's staff down to the rank of captain. Le Caron still had some sabotage to carry out, and would not have been courting attention.

The boundary between the two countries was marked by an iron post, and a Fenian sentry, Private John Rowe, was placed within a few yards of it. Bordering the road, the majority being on the United States side, were about two dozen family dwellings, some wooden stables and small barns, and a tannery. Running down the valley on the Canadian side, almost parallel to the boundary line and about 20 yards from it, was a fordable stream called Groat's Creek (or, locally, Chickabiddy Creek), spanned by a wooden bridge. Traffic delayed by the Fenian picket on the road was increasing when General Foster, accompanied by two deputies, rode down the road and stopped at the picket. After a brief wait they passed through and crossed into Canada to see Lieutenant-Colonel Chamberlin.

Aged 43, Chamberlin, commanding the Battalion of Volunteer Militia, was a rugged character with a large beard and moustache, a barrister turned journalist and a prominent public figure who three years earlier had been elected to sit for the County of Missisquoi in the first Parliament under Confederation. Foster related how he had summoned the Fenians, in the name of the United States Government, to lay down their arms and abandon their illegal marauding project, and how O'Neill had refused. He explained that he had no soldiers to enforce his demand but assured Chamberlin that United States troops were already on the way. Then he repeated O'Neill's message that the war would be conducted in a civilized fashion.

Outraged that an officer in United States uniform should carry a message from an outlaw who had defied the authority of the United States and was about to commit murder on British soil, Chamberlin refused to accept the message. It was scarcely satisfactory, he said, to those whom the Fenians intended to murder because they were in arms for the defence of their Government and country to know that this piracy would not be attended with unusual barbarities. His anger rose to the point where he threatened to arrest the American General on the charge of being a Fenian.

Chamberlin's irrational outburst expressed the widespread feeling on the Canadian side that the United States Government had been so complacent about the obvious Fenian preparations for the raid as to suggest sympathy with the rebels. The Marshal, in doing his best with his limited powers, was being snubbed by both sides. A diversion now occurred which ended the interview. The head of the

Fenian column was observed moving over the brow of the hill opposite and Chamberlin called his visitor's attention to it. Foster said: 'I thought they intended to attack you soon, but not so soon as this.' He rode back across the line and passed the Fenian column as he neared the rear of Vincent's house. Chamberlin, his force still considerably outnumbered although reinforcements were moving up from Stanbridge, made his dispositions to resist the attack, reserving for himself an exposed position in the centre which gave him a commanding view of the advancing enemy.

At the Fenian base O'Neill had given the order to fall in. The men who faced him were in a condition not unusual for soldiers going into battle—they were tired and their feet hurt. They had marched (as had the Canadian militia) through the deep mire of rain-sodden roads, the mud sucking at their boots, and now they were sweating in the heat. Now that the moment had come, however, they put on a good show. A Canadian journalist was impressed: 'As the Fenians came down the road, some 200 strong, they presented a rather formidable appearance; they marched with the steadiness of regular troops. They were nearly all in uniform and marched in column, with rifles at the "shoulder", with fixed bayonets, which shone and glistened in the noon-day sun, with a brightness that was dazzling.' The head of the column halted about 100 yards from the boundary, outside a house owned by Mr Alva Rykert. They loaded and O'Neill addressed them.

'Soldiers! This is the advance guard of the Irish-American army for the liberation of Ireland from the yoke of the oppressor. For your own country, you now enter that of the enemy. The eyes of your countrymen are upon you. Forward! March!'

Before the skirmishers went forward, Captain Cronan, commanding the advance company of forty men from Vermont, replied. 'General! I am proud that Vermont has the honour of leading this advance. Ireland may depend upon us to do our duty.'

The main body, under General Lewis, halted outside Rykert's house. Behind the hill was a reserve of about a hundred. Acting as though he were a commander with belligerent rights, O'Neill entered Rykert's house and went up to the attic to observe the action from the window.

'On to Canada!' The slogan had been chanted for years at excited demonstrations. Now the leading Fenians had only a few yards to go. Cheering wildly, they dashed down a gentle grassy slope into British territory. John Rowe, the sentry at the iron post, fell in with them. In close order they crossed the bridge and headed for the rocks and trees of Eccles Hill.

Another Fenian attack, under Generals Starr and Gleason, was mounted on the Huntingdon border. The operator at the South Hinchinbrook telegraph office tapped out the one word 'Goodbye' before a small advance party arrived. While his men helped themselves to 40 lbs of tobacco from Holbrooke's store, the leader started to wrench the telegraph instrument from its fastenings, but the operator explained to him that communication could as effectively be cut by severing the wires. The invaders advanced about a mile and a half along the line of the Trout River and dug themselves into a well-chosen position.

Scouts had kept the Fenians under observation and volunteer units from Quebec and Montreal were on the way.

Heavy traffic in cipher telegrams had been passing between London and Ottawa since the beginning of May. Now the Governor-General, Sir John Young, cabled Earl Granville at the Colonial Office in London: 'Fenians from St Albans have crossed our frontier near Phillipsburg skirmishing reported to have commenced various other points threatened all along frontier we called out militia again three days ago and made all possible preparations.'

A despatch was drafted for the Foreign Office to send to the United States Government calling attention to 'the gravity of the present state of affairs' on their northern frontier. As United States troops were already on the move, and General Foster was doing everything that could be expected of him, this message could have been little more than a formality.

Some Whitehall civil servant put a note on the file suggesting that reports in the United States newspapers were exaggerated.

The Fenians' cheers as they looked up to Eccles Hill were cut short by the staccato sound of rifle fire. Private John Rowe fell dead and Lieutenant John Hallinan staggered with a flesh wound in the arm. Smoke rose from behind the rocks and through the brushwood. The invaders were startled by the rapid fire and alarmed by the sight of the 60th Battalion's red jackets; they supposed they were facing British regulars. The following company, which they had thought to be close behind them, was still on United States territory and was firing from there. They wavered, recovered sufficiently to fire haphazardly in the direction of the rocks, and scattered to shelter behind barns and stone walls. As they turned, Captain Cronan was hit in the side. Staggering away, he called to a fellow officer to take command and keep the men together. Already the men were beyond taking orders. The main body on the road continued firing until the Canadians, whose shots at first went over their heads, found the range and men began to go down. General Lewis was hit in the leg, lifted from his horse and carried with other wounded into a house.

Civilian spectators sought refuge behind walls and buildings. An American reporter had his hat shot off and, according to other newspapermen, ran 3 miles without stopping. Farmers and teamsters from Vermont, waiting with empty waggons for the opportunity to move forward and collect the booty which was to repay them for transporting the Fenians' war supplies, found themselves under fire and moved back in a confused mass.

Officers of Cronan's company shouted appeals to the main force to come forward to support them. About fifty men advanced a few paces and fired towards Eccles Hill, but they too broke and took shelter. Some men proceeded to a hilltop wood opposite the Canadian position, one being killed and several wounded on the way.

In all this dangerous confusion there occurred an incident of the kind which stirred Victorian hearts and inspired British boys with military ambitions. In full view of the enemy, regardless of the whistling bullets, Colonel Osborne Smith galloped along the road and up Eccles Hill, to be received at the top with the cheers of his men. He had left Eccles Hill with a Captain Gascoigne that morning, when there was no immediate prospect of an attack, to bring up Montreal volunteers from Stanbridge. When within 2 miles of Stanbridge he had been overtaken by a mounted messenger from Lieutenant-Colonel Chamberlin, who informed him that the Fenians were on the point of attacking. Colonel Smith thereupon sent the captain on to Stanbridge, with instructions to collect every available man, and hastened back to Eccles Hill. There he found Lieutenant-Colonel Chamberlin, no less gallant, holding the most exposed and dangerous position, and there he assumed command.

69

Canadian riflemen, suspecting that Rykert's house was being used as the Fenian General's headquarters, directed their fire at it. Angered at the damage being done to his property, the owner went upstairs and ordered his unwelcome tenant to leave at once. Accounts differ about what went on in the attic, but O'Neill eventually submitted to the indignity and appeared at the back door. There he addressed the men who were sheltering behind the house and a lumber pile. He is recorded as saying:

> Men of Ireland! I am ashamed of you. You have acted disgracefully, but you will have another chance of showing whether you are cravens or not. Comrades, we must not, *we dare not*, go back now, with the stain of cowardice upon us. Comrades, I will lead you again, and if you will not follow me, I will go on with my officers and die in your front. I leave you now under command of General Boyle O'Reilly.

O'Neill was never at a loss for a speech, but this utterance seems rather improbable. Who made a note of it in those circumstances, and to how many was he audible? Was he referring to Ridgeway in 1866 when he said, 'I will lead you again', and did his audience understand that he was about to lead them in a death or glory charge up the hill? He had to endure heckling by furious men who had been assured that the only Canadian opposition would come from a few unorganized farmers. The General retorted that the hill was being held by not more than fifty Canadian militiamen, but the sight of the red coats and the rapidity and accuracy of the fire had convinced his soldiers that they were pitted against British troops. Private James Keenan provided an example of the defence's effectiveness by venturing a few paces beyond the shelter of the house and promptly collapsing from a bullet just above the ankle. Seeing that the men were not to be rallied, O'Neill ordered them to keep on firing, and he set an example by getting behind a lumber pile and shooting at a Canadian officer who was in an exposed position on the hill.

A few minutes after this demonstration of aggression a closed carriage came down the road and stopped in the shelter of Rykert's house. General Foster, whom O'Neill had received so ungraciously at the Franklin Hotel that morning, alighted, put his hand on O'Neill's shoulder, and formally arrested him for a breach of the Neutrality Act. The Marshal's assistant, Mr Smalley, took O'Neill by the arm. One version of this incident has Foster holding a pistol to the Fenian leader's head but others present record that O'Neill merely threatened to call upon his men to rescue him. 'He did not do so, however,' wrote a reporter, 'and as he was hurried past a group of them and one or two officers, they looked on with about as much interest as if they were watching the performance of a burlesque on a historical drama.' Accompanied by his captors, O'Neill stepped into the carriage. The horses started off at a smart pace on the road to St Albans, which led past the Fenian camp.

The 400 men for whom Le Caron had been waiting had now arrived. Showing no desperate haste, weary and hot, they had drawn their equipment and, at half-past one, they were forming into line on the public road. Their heads turned and they shuffled back hurriedly on hearing a cry: 'Clear the road! Clear the road!' A carriage drawn by furiously galloping horses lurched by. Le Caron glimpsed the downcast face of O'Neill. 'I understood the situation in a moment,' he recalls, 'but said nothing. To have given the command to shoot the horses as they turned would have been the work of an instant, but it was not part of my purpose to restore O'Neill to his command.'

Contingents were now belatedly arriving but, as the news spread of O'Neill's removal from the scene, no one knew what to do. Firing could be heard from the direction of Chickabiddy Creek. All the available senior officers assembled in a glade near Hubbard's Farm. Standing in a circle, their troops looking on, they held a council of war. General John Boyle O'Reilly, a man of average build, with a bronzed face, moustache and goatee beard, wearing a dark green jacket elaborately ornamented with yellow braid, who enjoyed great prestige as an Irish patriot, was asked to take command and mount an attack at some other point, but he could see no purpose in starting an operation elsewhere and he refused to be prevailed upon.

By this time the Canadians were visibly reinforcing their position. A troop of cavalry trotted along the road and up the hill and a rifle company arrived in waggons. The Fenians continued firing, with varying intensity, until about three o'clock, when they hung out a white flag in front of Rykert's dwelling and several women came out of houses near the line. Firing from the Canadian side ceased but Colonel Smith forbade his volunteers to leave their positions. About fifteen of the home guards went down to the boundary to meet a

71

dozen Fenians headed by O'Reilly. He shouted that they wanted a short pause to remove their dead and wounded, and requested to speak to a Canadian officer. One of the home guards went back to Colonel Smith and repeated the request. In the meantime spectators emerged from their places of safety and swarmed down to the boundary. Colonel Smith refused to have any communication with the Fenian General and ordered the home guards back to their posts. An altercation was in progress between the two parties, O'Reilly being taunted for seeking petticoat protection by inducing the women to come out, and he threatening to fire if the home guards removed Rowe's body to their side, which some were proposing to do. After waiting about ten minutes O'Reilly, needing a face-saving gesture, called out at the top of his voice: 'As your officer will not send any answer, all stragglers had better quit this, for just so soon as you get into proper range we will open fire again.' The bystanders ran for cover and the opposing parties retreated to their positions, leaving Rowe's body where it lay. The Fenians then fired a few shots, and a lull ensued, during which the Canadian defenders were able to eat the biscuits and butter sent by Frelighsburg residents.

At Hubbard's Farm about 100 men of the New York Irish, under Major Moore, had arrived. Having missed the action, they were determined on a demonstration, and shortly after four o'clock they opened a heavy fire from the brow of the hill. Fenians trapped in houses along the road joined in. At the same time some of Major Moore's men moved a field-piece down through the woods and positioned it to fire on the volunteer camp. It seemed that a battle was about to start. Major Moore ordered an advance but his men, who knew that cavalry were protecting the flanks, who were convinced that they would face regular soldiers, and who had heard rumours that a field battery was on Eccles Hill, openly disobeyed and withdrew to Franklin Centre.

In the early evening firing nearly ceased on both sides. Farm carts appeared on the road and civilians emerged. Some of the Fenians still concealed in the houses took off their uniforms, abandoned their arms and made their way back to the camp. Colonel Smith then learned that a detachment of the enemy with a field-piece was in the valley on the right and he ordered an advance. Seeing the approaching Canadians some of the Fenians fired, but as the defenders came on, firing as they advanced, the invaders broke cover and, throwing away their weapons, retreated in what a reporter called 'a regular skedaddle'. A few shots were fired from behind the hill but none fell near the Canadian camp.

After dark lights were seen as the Fenians searched for their dead and wounded. Four or five had been killed and about fifteen (including General Donnely) wounded. During the engagement not a single Canadian was even wounded.

In New York a large assembly at the Hibernian Hall cheered wildly as a telegram was read that the Fenian army had crossed the border.

At headquarters, however, there was no unanimity. James Gibbons, President of the Senate of the Fenian Brotherhood, repudiated the raid as premature and unauthorized.

Officers and men at Hubbard's Farm waited through the night for someone who would tell them what to do. When General Spier, the Secretary of War of the Fenian Brotherhood, and his aide-de-camp, Colonel Brown, arrived on the following morning, the force had dwindled in numbers. Unable to bring themselves to admit defeat, the two officers appealed for more weapons and ammunition to be distributed and for the attack to be resumed. But rumours were circulating of the imminent arrival of United States troops; with the threat of arrest and imprisonment for a breach of the Neutrality Act, the men facing them were wondering how best to get home. Within a few hours they had abandoned their camp and left behind substantial quantities of arms, ammunition and clothing, which were seized by United States troops who appeared not long after. Canadian soldiers clearing the scene of combat acquired a lot of abandoned arms and accoutrements and the field-piece, which the Missisquoi home guard kept as a trophy.

The force under Generals Starr and Gleason left its defensive position on 26 May, on learning of O'Neill's defeat, and withdrew to the American side. On the following day, however, it reoccupied the same position until driven from it by a Canadian bayonet charge. So exultant were the Canadian troops that they had to be restrained from pursuing the invaders on to United States territory. The two generals were arrested at St Albans.

When the news of the repulses at Eccles Hill and Trout River reached Buffalo, Detroit and other places where Fenians had congregated with the intention of crossing the frontier in the wake of the army of the Irish Republic they dispersed.

During the break-up of the camp at Hubbard's Farm, Le Caron continued to behave inconspicuously. When his associates were, for want of any other plan, leaving for the assembly centre at Malone (where they were to find similar demoralization), Le Caron announced that he was going to Burlington to see what could be done about O'Neill. Charged with violating the Neutrality Act, and unable to find bail of $20,000, the General was being held in gaol there.

Actually, Le Caron set out to go by a devious route to Ottawa. By way of Rouses Point he went to Montreal. He stayed a night with Judge Coursel, the Commissioner of the Quebec Police, and the next morning took the train to Ottawa, which made a scheduled half-hour stop for a meal at Cornwall.

While he was eating his dinner, a tall military-looking man and a preacher entered the station dining room together. The cleric pointed to Le Caron and said: 'That is the man.'

The tall man approached Le Caron, put his hand on his shoulder, and said: 'You are my prisoner!'

10

Badly Cheated

Perhaps the unkindest comment on O'Neill's performance came from the members of the St Albans Brotherhood, who accused the General of having arranged before the battle for his own arrest. Embittered men, with little money, hung about the town, sleeping in the streets, not knowing how they were to get home. In the oppressive heat thirsts became acute—a condition which greatly facilitates the task of reporters wanting comments. The representative of the *Ottawa Times* wrote: 'The men charge their failure to the inefficiency and cowardice of their officers. They say that they were anxious to charge the Canadians on the hill, but were not allowed to do so. The officers certainly voted the retreat and many of them are now invisible to the naked eye.'

A man who visited Malone described 'a lot of straggling and discouraged scamps who say they have been badly cheated'. So anxious were the municipal authorities to rid themselves of this nuisance that they supported a proposal to send the Fenians home in boxcars at half price by offering to contribute part of the fare. In the following week 1,150 tickets were issued. Within the Fenian movement generally such confusion existed that while the destitute troops were being moved south, a party of 150 from Boston was on its way north to support the invading army.

Observers of the total demoralization were inclined, prematurely as it turned out, to write the Irish-American Fenian movement off. 'The Fenian movement has utterly died out,' wrote the *Ottawa Citizen*. 'Most of the wretched dupes have gone away from the frontier, all who could do so by any means, and those who remain are making Fenianism stink in the nostrils of their American sympathizers.' The *Globe* commented:

> The raid on Canada is over. A wilful and persistent misrepresentation has characterized the whole affair from the beginning. The statement that the United States Government would sympathize with the advance on Canada was constantly preached to men in their circles, and it was asserted that at least 15,000 Fenians would assemble on the Canadian frontier. . . . Now the men know the deception that was practised, and are outspoken against the men who deceived them.

After the Fenians had decamped from the Huntingdon border American and Canadian residents hurried to see the base. Among them was the editor of the local paper, the *Gleaner*, whose account pays an unwitting tribute to Le Caron's efficiency in equipping the Fenian army and helps to explain O'Neill's faith in him as a military administrator.

> It passes all belief the quantity of stores of every kind which had been accumulated, and we think we are below the truth in stating that a quarter of a million dollars would not pay for all that was sent to the frontier. There were boxes of rifles, boxes of bayonets, boxes of water bottles, boxes of knapsacks and haversacks, boxes of belts, and boxes of clothing; besides these, there were barrels of pork and hard tack. In short, the most wonderful part of the movement was the completeness and extent of the preparations, for all of which, we hold, the United States Government is responsible. To say that such a quantity of stores and arms could be prepared and sent to the frontier without its knowledge is absurd. The New York *Tribune*, and other papers, laughed at the Fenians as an army without a commissariat; but the truth is, it was a splendid commissariat without an army worthy of it.

In their collective summing-up, Canadian journalists, describing petty quarrelling and indiscipline as characteristic of the Fenian force, wrote:

> Such a state of affairs was very discouraging to the more respectable among them, for all were not roughs and blackguards, as one

might suppose, judging from the desperate and piratical nature of their enterprise. Many were respectable laborers and mechanics, whose enthusiasm, fired at the thought of in some way freeing Ireland from the Saxon rule, had overridden their judgment, or who, having long been connected with the Brotherhood, had been urged forward to the step by a fear of shame, lest they should be accused of cowardice if they now shirked action. These were the minority, however; the greater part were the off-scourings of city populations, adventurers, rowdies and ne'er-do-wells, who had been lured by the prospect of plunder, and were only restrained, during their short stay in camp, by the fear that excesses or outrages there might bring down upon them the American authorities, a result they were very anxious to avoid.

Judge McMicken, in a report to the Canadian military authorities, described the result of the attack as the 'utter demoralization of the Fenian body and the perfect prostration of their hopes'.

General agreement existed that the repulse of the attack had been good for Canadian morale. Commanding officers addressing the troops, mayors welcoming the boys back home, Lieutenant-General the Honourable James Lindsay in his General Order to the volunteers, all pursued the same theme, that the voluntary militia of the new dominion had proved itself and that the Canadian people had gained reliance on themselves.

The London *Times* gave less attention to the attack than it had to the attempted invasion four years previously and its comment on 27 May was contemptuous: 'Fenianism is now merely an organization maintained by a few rogues for their own benefit, and it is not to be tolerated that they should pursue this trade at the cost of the lives and the property of British subjects and the annoyance of a friendly nation.' In its next issue it characterized the Fenians as lawless gangs, ruffians and brawlers.

Nobody came forward with $20,000 to secure O'Neill's release on bail from prison in Burlington. The now disgraced hero of Ridgeway was to stay there for the next six months, and he might have reflected that he was well out of the way for the time being.

During this retreat from public life he conceived another plan.

11

Under Arrest

At first Le Caron did not realize the seriousness of his position.
Thinking that the two men had mistaken him for somebody else, he
laughed, asked 'What's the matter?' and turned to resume his meal.
But the tall man, whose accent which revealed that he, or at least
his parents, came from Scotland, looked at him stolidly, repeated
his first statement, and added: 'You must come with me at once.'

A brief argument ensued.

'But won't you let me finish my dinner?'

'No. Come.'

'For what reason? Why am I arrested?'

Then came the accusation which startled the other passengers in
the dining room. 'You are a Fenian.'

Angry murmurs from the onlookers now became audible. Le
Caron jumped up and accompanied the two men to a room adjoining
the ticket office. The tall man, it was now revealed, was the mayor.
The man in the clerical attire was an itinerant preacher who had
been in Malone when Le Caron was there supervising the distribution of arms. Le Caron had been pointed out to him as the
leading Fenian agent and he had remembered his appearance.

Faced with arrest and possible lynching, Le Caron could only take
the mayor into his confidence and hope to be believed, so he asked to
talk to him alone. He explained that, although appearing as a
Fenian, he was a government agent on his way to see Judge
McMicken, and he suggested that the mayor should allow him to
travel on to Ottawa under guard and send the Judge a telegram

announcing his arrival. Le Caron's convincing manner, which had made his under-cover career possible, saved him on this occasion. The mayor put him in the charge of a Canadian lieutenant who was returning with a party from the scene of the invasion. This officer installed him in a carriage guarded by a sergeant and two soldiers. They shut the windows and, to his dismay, ordered him to put his cigar out. As the story that a Fenian had been captured spread through the train, the escort saw that its main task was to protect the prisoner from hostile groups shouting 'Hang him' or 'Lynch him' rather than to prevent his escape.

The news circulated so rapidly that at Prescott Junction a Toronto *Globe* reporter was waiting, but Le Caron refused to say anything. Hungry, and feeling the tobacco addict's craving, he put his hand time and again on his cigar case, only to occasion a roar from the sergeant. He spent the journey in a state of resentment and discomfort, expecting to be released as soon as the train arrived at Ottawa.

Judge McMicken's representative was at the station as though to meet an ordinary prisoner. Led by this man, the guards hustled him to the police office, and stood over him. Le Caron seems to have felt outraged by this treatment; he appears not to have grasped that to the soldiers he was a prisoner for whose safe delivery they were responsible. It was not in his nature to act the role of a wretched captive, and it must have needed self-restraint not to declare his identity.

When he was escorted before Judge McMicken he laughed, but the Judge regarded the arrivals gravely and adhered to the formalities. Le Caron was still only 29. To him the Judge, then 56, seemed an old man, and he was subdued by the sense of awe which his professional behaviour imposed on the proceedings. McMicken unhurriedly studied a paper and listened to the evidence of arrest. Then he signed the receipt for the live body of the prisoner, handed it to the sergeant and told him that he and his men could withdraw. Not until the soldiers had gone did the Judge smile. At last Le Caron could smoke. The two men sat talking until McMicken thought it was dark enough outside for them to emerge. Then he called a cab and they drove to his club.

What followed is a surprising episode in the life of a secret agent. Here is Le Caron's account of it:

In the club the Fenian prisoner of a few hours previously was made a most welcome guest, and had an exceedingly good time. My identity being known to some of the officers who crowded the club-house after their return from Franklin, I found myself quite the hero of the hour, and had most interesting chats over the experiences of the raid on both sides of the fight.

The euphoria of that night at the club is easily imagined—the anecdotes told in penetrating military voices, the chaff and back-slapping laughter, the frequent toasts and the dense cigar smoke. Although Le Caron would have refused the drinks pressed upon him, he would not have opted out of the conversation. The convivial company gave him the recognition which was what, above all, he yearned for. After years of playing a part, of discreetly supporting whatever was the ruling opinion in the Fenian Brotherhood, of associating with men he despised, he was now among his own people on the right side, relieved that they knew him and appreciated what he had done. It is puzzling that McMicken did not conclude that his principal agent's cover was now blown and that he must get his man into hiding without delay. A club is not a place where members and servants can be sworn to secrecy. Surely this revelation of the spy from within the enemy's camp was too good a story not to be retailed to friends and wives, who would in their turn pass it on to others.

That night he slept at the club. McMicken, now showing caution, decided that Le Caron must not return home by the same route, and arranged for him to be driven during the night to Ann Prior terminus, some forty miles from Ottawa. From there he was to take a branch line. As he had insufficient funds to get home, and no one on the premises could raise enough cash, McMicken sent the club porter to fetch some money; Le Caron recalls the sum as $350 but McMicken charged it in his expenses account as $250. The amount was sufficiently large to impress the porter, who gossiped about the transaction.

A rather vague story got into the Canadian press to the effect that immediately after the raid an important Fenian had appeared in Ottawa to be paid a large sum by a government official. It concluded with a comment that the Fenians must have been duped.

12

The Judge's Assessment

With the Fenian movement supposedly shattered, the time had come for the Canadian Government to settle its debt to Le Caron. In the course of briefing the Prime Minister, McMicken wrote two letters assessing his agent's services and character. They confirm Le Caron's subsequent claims as to the importance of his work and reveal that he slowed up the Fenian offensive. McMicken knew Le Caron as a working spy better than anyone, and the picture he gives of him differs widely from the man's own presentation of himself and the impression he gave later as a public figure.

The first letter was written, as always, in the Judge's own handwriting and not by a clerk, on 7 July 1870.

> Permit me then to say first of all in reference to H. Le Caron that I entered into an arrangement with him in June 1868—so that he has been employed for 2 years. During this period he has devoted himself to the service and performed it (from my point of view) zealously, faithfully and to great advantage for the Public interests.
>
> Taking into account the sums at different times paid to him in cases of exigency he has received from me for the period of his service an average salary of $100 per month. The understanding had with him was that when occasion should arise to dispense with his services their value and faithfulness should be taken into account and such liberal sum paid him as the Government should deem proper.
>
> To him we are largely if not altogether indebted for the very

precise information of the movement plan of campaign and state of preparation &c.

When the movement **did** take place his personal services in antagonism to Fenian operations were highly advantageous in furthering the result which occurred. He rendered the only gun the Fenians had unserviceable by removing the breechpiece and concealing it so that it could not be found for several hours after the repulse of the invading body under O'Neill, thereby probably saving lives and disaster to the few volunteers on the ground.

He also delayed or caused the delay in bringing up the reserve force of Fenians some 400 strong to the support of O'Neill for about 2 hours instead of some 20 minutes and thereby contributed to the discomfiture of O'Neill and the collapse of the movement. He is now bitterly denounced by the Fenian newspapers—not however as a traitor—but as a hired tool of O'Neill's without heart in the cause and not an Irishman chiefly blamed for his disregard of their war material and for inviting the country people around to help themselves to arms &c. Of his personal safety to which I've alluded I have always been especially careful and if [he] ever encountered any risk or is subject to any now it is entirely owing to his own imprudence which he will readily admit—he is very excitable and very fond of having it known that he was a great instrument of discomfiture to the Fenians—that although unfaithful to them he was a true-hearted Englishman and had no sympathy but utter detestation of them and their designs and would when there was no occasion whatever for it reveal his name and occupation to parties who would not and should not have known anything of the kind.

In whatever light his real character should be viewed he certainly has acted faithfully, zealously and ably in carrying out the work undertaken by him in serving British and Canadian interests in preparing us for Fenian hostilities &c.

He says he must of necessity move away from where he has been residing and urgently pleads necessity for an immediate remittance of the sum to be given him in settlement.

He has never named any sum on which his expectations rested but my impression is he will not feel satisfied with less than £500—or $2,000. I am inclined to think he calculates on something considerably in excess of this.

In the following communication, dated 6 July, a sentence is quoted from a letter written by Le Caron to one of McMicken's sons in the police department regretting an unexplained indiscretion. It is possible that the 'wise old judge' (Le Caron's phrase) curbed his exuberance at the Ottawa party. Evidently there had been some anxiety, and McMicken's concern to absolve himself from blame if his agent were exposed might imply that he thought that the revelations at the club and the subsequent newspaper hints might open Fenian eyes and provoke vengeance. The letter ran:

> As to his personal safety I have never ceased to exercise the strictest circumspection and care but he is of a very mercurial and excitable temperament and has often acted very indiscreetly and imprudently and has on several occasions called into exercise my best judgement to relieve him from difficulties by way of exposure of his own making. To quote his own words in a letter written by him to my son on 21st ult.: 'I am glad the affair has blown over so quietly, it needed a little of your father's cool brain to prevent my making a fool of myself.' It will appear that he can have no cause to apprehend any trouble from indiscretion on my part or of anyone knowing him or of him through me. He communicated to 4 or 5 of my force freely all about himself, his proper name, his position and standing with the Fenians and nature of his agreement with me, all of which was entirely unnecessary and contrary to my injunctions of caution to him,—however, I believe he has so far escaped suspicion as an actual traitor to them but he is blamed as a heartless tool of O'Neill's, not being an Irishman having no interest in the cause and upon the failure of the movement instead of doing what he could to save the war material and actually inviting the country people to come in and help themselves.
>
> I doubt much that he can ever regain the position amongst them of any great usefulness to us and there is always the danger existing of an exposure of his character by some act of inadvertence or wilfulness on the part of some of those individuals to whom he so unnecessarily exposed himself.

Inevitably, treasury minds saw the minimum of $2,000 as the maximum, although McMicken wrote a note that Le Caron 'figures up his losses and services as $5,000'. The lower sum, which he accepted without argument, became his official award, and the amount was entered in McMicken's papers with the statement that Le Caron had also received £50 sterling from the British Government. (Anderson later remarked on another, unspecified, grant that though 'petty in comparison with the value of his services, it was, at least, substantial'.) William Montgomery, alias McMichael, the New York contact, was paid $300 bonus and kept on at $60 a month. Mr Archibald, the British Consul in New York, was to retain his Fenian informer so that there would be two sources of intelligence which could be checked one against the other. The remaining principal agent, J. M. McDonald, was paid off with $200.

Then came the usual civil service hiatus between decision and action. As weeks passed and no money arrived, the agents felt themselves forgotten and they complained to McMicken. In future, it had just been arranged, such payments would come from the Secret Service Fund instead of McMicken's Public Accounts and Police Expenditure, so he in turn appealed to Colonel Bernard at military headquarters. His letter dated 1 August reveals the sad aftermath which Le Caron was now experiencing.

> During the past month I have had several letters from Le Caron in all of which he represents himself as in most deplorable circumstances and begs piteously for a settlement and remittance. I give an extract from 2:
>
> 'I have only to say in answer to yours that *here* I am in a little Hell on Earth and am anxiously awaiting the time when I can clear out. I do not want to sell off everything I have at a great loss and have not the money to get away.
>
> 'I must ask you as a favour to send me a small sum of money by return of Post which I am very much in need of, deducting it if you choose from the money which you will pay me in settlement.
>
> 'I do not care to be a beggar and if I had a dollar to help myself I would not ask you in this way.'

McMicken sent him $20, all the funds he had available from the previous month, and asked Colonel Bernard—spontaneous generosity not coming within the rules—if the amount was to be deducted from the $2,000.

Fenians who had been too slow in the retreat to avoid being caught by the Canadians were now trickling back. Ninety-eight had been captured. Most of them received sentences of imprisonment of from three weeks to eight months. Twenty-two were sentenced to death but the sentences were commuted to imprisonment. Considering the enormity of an armed attack on their territory, the Canadians cannot be said to have been vindictive. O'Neill, brought before a United States court, had also come off lightly; in a sense, his sentence of only six months was yet another indignity. Yet his confidence in his powers of persuasion, his conviction that men would trustingly follow him into battle, were undiminished.

In 1871 Le Caron was again reporting on O'Neill.

13

The Usual Drill

Unrest among the half-breeds (known as Metis) in the north-west was one of McMicken's many concerns, and he had their leader, Louis Riel, under observation. Le Caron was now devoting himself mainly to his medical studies, which had been so dramatically interrupted, but he still held his position in the Fenian movement, and his reports occasionally mentioned Riel as the subject of discussion among the Senate of the Brotherhood. Riel hoped that the Irish-Americans might aid him against their common enemy by supplying men and arms. His appeal, however, was inopportune. After the costly fiasco at Eccles Hill the movement for Irish independence was disorganized and impoverished, and most of its leaders were in no mood to equip an expedition to support the rebellious offspring of whites and American Indians in far-off Manitoba.

O'Neill disagreed with the majority. Following his often-expressed policy of 'anything to cripple the enemy', he campaigned to raise yet another Fenian force for an attack on the dominion. He was not interested in the cause of the Metis; he had seen service against the Red Indians in the far west, and claims to purity of race heightened the fervour at Irish gatherings, where the term half-breed could be used as an insult. The somewhat listless response of audiences to his appeals, so like those they had heard before with their assurances of vast numbers of hospitable Metis waiting to welcome the liberators from the south, did not deter him from going ahead with the project.

To obtain the necessary arms and ammunition he called on his trusted friend Le Caron, bringing documents to prove the genuineness of the rebel movement's intentions. Le Caron read, to his 'amazement and disgust', as he recorded, that aid was being solicited by a young priest, the Reverend W. B. O'Donahoe, who claimed to have his bishop's permission to abandon his clerical garments and assist Riel. The correspondence was in Le Caron's possession long enough for him to make copies for Whitehall and Ottawa. In his other capacity he conducted O'Neill to a hidden depository at Port Huron in Michigan where lay a stock of the breech loaders converted at an inflated cost from Springfield rifles in the Trenton armoury. Originally O'Neill asked for 400 rifles, which Le Caron agreed to supply, but eventually he took 250.

Recently McMicken had been appointed Agent of Dominion Lands for Manitoba in addition to his other offices. Continuing news during 1871 of the disturbed state of public feeling in the province caused him to leave Ottawa to visit Fort Garry, the centre of the trouble, after instructing his agents in the United States to meet him in Chicago. While making a stop at his home in Windsor to settle family affairs he received a telegram from the Premier urging him to hurry on. Accompanied by his son George and Frank Ritchie, both members of his Secret Service Police, he took the train to Chicago. Between connections he met Le Caron and other contacts. By the time he resumed the journey he knew that O'Neill had enlisted only forty-one volunteers, that they were short of money, and that their first object was to loot the Hudson Bay Company's stores at Pembina and Fort Garry early in October.

It was now nearing the end of September and McMicken's destination lay several difficult days' journey away. He and his two companions carried pistols; he also took a new sporting rifle and a handsome Irish retriever—both gifts from friends. They boarded the train for St Paul, going by way of McGregor and Prairie du Chien. A wait of two days in St Paul ensued before they could proceed on the Breckenridge Railway, then under construction. Where the line terminated, at a point known as Morris, the temporary station building constituted the sole accommodation and travellers slept, as the Judge put it, '40 for a garret'. Here they met the other five passengers, all business men, who had booked to travel by stage to Fort Garry.

After supper the stage vehicle from Fort Garry arrived, bringing

Bishop Tache, O'Donahoe's superior. An affable character, the Bishop readily answered McMicken's questions about the situation there. The Metis, he said, were intensely agitated over unfulfilled government promises and the harsh and insulting conduct of Canadians recently arrived from Ontario, especially of the volunteers who were so hostile and abusive as to provoke severe retaliation. At an overnight stop on the way he had met O'Donahoe moving in the other direction and had tried to persuade him to venture no further, but the young priest had maintained that he was going in with friends who intended to take up homesteads as peaceful settlers. McMicken in vain urged Tache (who had an important appointment in Quebec) to return to Fort Garry with him, as the Bishop's presence there would help to preserve peace. The Judge spent the night writing a duplicate coded despatch for Ottawa, one to be sent by the station telegraph operator and the other to be handed in by the Bishop at St Paul telegraph office.

The coach started at six o'clock. At the first change of horses, about two and a half hours later, McMicken tried out his new gun by sighting it on a small swimming bird to see how the shot would strike the water. At the sound as he pulled the trigger the retriever bolted and disappeared in the prairie without a backward glance.

During stops every 12 or 15 miles on the route McMicken and his two companions gathered information about Fenian movements and conditions at Fort Garry. One fellow passenger, Mr Wylie, travelling for the firm of James Turner & Company, of Hamilton, knew everybody along the road and indicated to the Judge who was likely to be well informed. At Macaulayville the landlady, the possessor of (in McMicken's words) 'a loving and loyal Canadian heart', had overheard Bishop Tache's talk with the priest, and she confirmed that the Bishop had endeavoured to dissuade the young man from the enterprise. A party of local Fenians, she related, who had just paraded sporting green ribbons, were to leave the next day to attack Fort Garry. Frank Ritchie learned from an old army comrade he encountered that two waggons with armed men, 'a rough hard looking set', had recently encamped for the night while making their way to Pembina to meet other parties. This information caused McMicken some anxiety. He asked Mr Wylie to persuade the stage agent to rebook the coach as an express for the rest of the way. The agent made difficulties, but an extra fee of $500 induced him to agree. A new waybill for eight persons was made out in Wylie's name only, as the name of McMicken would put the party in danger.

Ahead of them, waiting for the stage at Grand Forks, was a Mr Pearson. He was horrified to hear a man telling a group of thirteen or fourteen persons that Mr McMicken, the Receiver-General of Manitoba, was on his way in by stage carrying a million dollars with him. This man, whose name turned out to be Goldie, remarked that if there was any truth in what was being said about the trouble at Fort Garry, he felt awfully sorry for McMicken. The talkative Goldie had left Morris two days before the police party; having learned their destination and guessed their purpose, he gossiped about them to his fellow passengers—a married couple and two men, O'Donahoe and O'Neill.

At Georgetown Pearson saw Wylie descending from the coach. Rushing towards him, he asked if Mr McMicken was a passenger. Wylie hesitated.

'Wylie, this is no child's matter!' Pearson said. 'I ask you on the square if Mr McMicken is with you. It means for him life or death, and my anxiety is to save him from the danger which lies in his way.'

As McMicken emerged, Pearson exclaimed: 'You must on no account go any further, but return the way you came. You will be robbed and killed to a certainty!'

Pearson repeated what he had heard of Goldie's conversation and added that on the way there he had seen two waggons laden with barrels and arms, convoyed by 'villainous cut-throat ragamuffins'. He emphasized his warning: 'You won't attempt to go on. No, no, you must go back. You can do nothing to save yourself in this wild lone country—to proceed would be self-murder.'

McMicken did not underestimate the danger. As he said later, 'a couple of men on horseback armed with repeaters could have made us an easy prey.' Coolly he calculated the risks, working out where the Fenians would be at that time and estimating that his coachload should be safe for the next sixty-two miles. A prairie fire, flames of from 6 to 12 feet coming dangerously close, delayed them and blackened their faces and clothing. Mr Trail, the Hudson Bay Company's representative at Grand Forks, said that the Fenians had left about four hours previously and advised them to go no further. They took the precaution of leaving most of their money and some of their baggage behind for safe keeping, having had to exchange their roomy four-horse coach for a two-horse canvas-covered vehicle known as a jerky, in which they were uncomfortably crushed. They slipped past the Fenians' waggons in the dark. During the next stage they found themselves behind an Irish-American driver who had been sworn in as a Fenian two weeks before, so they pretended to be sympathetic Americans while he complained that the leaders of the revolt were attacking prematurely before adding consolingly: 'You'll see fun anyhow.'

They entered Pembina at dawn. Knowing that the occupants of the preceding coach would be sleeping at the inn, McMicken asked Wylie to find out from the proprietor, Robertson, which room Goldie was occupying. His face begrimed from the prairie fire, and pointing a revolver, the Judge burst into the room. Goldie, just buttoning his braces, was terrified. In violent language McMicken accused the trembling man of putting him in extreme danger. If he showed any recognition of him by word or deed, McMicken threatened, he would shoot him dead, and he ordered Goldie not to go out of his sight. Downstairs Goldie was still so frightened that he could scarcely hold his coffee cup. It was as well that he kept silent because, sitting at the other end of the stove from McMicken, was O'Donahoe. The raiders were to assemble at Pembina before marching on Fort Garry.

The party left without arousing suspicion. The journey was slow, the meals at the inns could be swallowed only (as McMicken put it) with 'starvation sauce', and when at sunset on Monday, 2 October, they arrived at Fort Garry they found in the Davis hotel 'nothing inviting, everything forbidding—dirt, discomfort and whiskey abundant'. Since leaving St Paul four and a half days earlier McMicken had slept for less than four hours, he was hungry and smoke-blackened. While eating a fried egg and a boiled potato, he was summoned by the chief of provincial police, in gold lace and spangles, to see the Lieutenant-Governor, Mr Archibald, at Government House.

Bedraggled as he was, and with his introductory letters left behind at Grand Forks, McMicken was warmly welcomed by Mr Archibald who, as he confessed, could not cope with the hostility of the Canadians and the Metis to each other and to himself personally. The Canadians in particular were malignantly antagonistic to the Lieutenant-Governor. Only seventy armed volunteers were at his disposal. He asked McMicken, as an experienced administrator, what he should do.

In his advice, which was in effect to follow the usual drill, the Judge provided an example of the magnificent bluff which made it possible for a world-wide empire to be governed from a small island in the North Sea. Without any hesitation, McMicken told him to issue a proclamation, in the Queen's name, calling the people to arms. Archibald, knowing the strength of local feeling and Riel's popular appeal, doubted whether a mere proclamation would receive a hearty response, but he had no other proposal. By midnight the two men were handing the draft to a printer, and he, by morning, had produced in a variety of types a poster bearing the Royal Arms over a greeting from Victoria to her loving subjects, the inhabitants of the Province of Manitoba. The language was majestic.

> Whereas, intelligence has just been received from trustworthy sources that a band of lawless men calling themselves FENIANS have assembled on the frontier at or near Pembina and that they intend to make a raid into this province, from a country with which we are at peace, and to commit acts of depredation, pillage and robbery, and other outrages upon the persons and property of our loving subjects, the inhabitants of this province.
> . . .

To repel this outrage the loving subjects, 'irrespective of race or religion, or of past local differences', were exhorted to 'RALLY ROUND THE FLAG of our common country', and to enrol to defend their homes and families.

The trick worked so well that even McMicken was astonished. On the following evening an enthusiastic public meeting expressed its loyalty, and within forty-eight hours over a thousand men (including some of Archibald's most virulent opponents) had volunteered for service. Where they came from, in that sparsely inhabited area, mystified McMicken. The extent of the response proved an embarrassment, because the Lieutenant-Governor disposed of only 650 rifles and those not allocated a weapon felt aggrieved. Over-enthusiasm on the part of the printer, in his role as captain of the home guard, led to the arrest of several persons for no better reason than that they were Roman Catholics and bore Irish names, and McMicken had to exercise his authority to release them from the police station cells.

91

A force moved off but did not need to go into action. The Canadian authorities had previously agreed that United States troops could if necessary cross the border to suppress a violation of the Neutrality Law. An American Army detachment arrested O'Neill, O'Donahoe and a small group of followers just as they started to rifle the Hudson Bay Company's stores. In a meaningless gesture, once the attempted invasion had failed Riel and some of his Metis offered their services to the Lieutenant-Governor.

The prisoners were taken back to the United States. When they appeared before a court at St Paul they were released on the grounds that they were charged with acts committed on British territory and therefore the court had no jurisdiction.

Le Caron, who claimed the credit for the collapse of the enterprise, did not appreciate the constitutional propriety of the acquittal; he considered it was arrived at on a 'ludicrous technicality'.

14

The Man with Two Keys

As a refuge from the 'little Hell on Earth', Le Caron—the Canadian Government having at last paid his bonus—chose Detroit. He sought the anonymity possible in a larger town, and Detroit offered two advantages: the College of Medicine, where he resumed his medical studies, and the presence of a bookseller named Mackey Lomasney, on whom McMicken was anxious to obtain reports.

Shopkeepers are an easy assignment for a secret agent, as they welcome all comers. Le Caron took to calling in to look at Lomasney's books and become acquainted with him. This 28-year-old Irishman had a police record. Although acquitted of the murder of a policeman in Ireland, he had been sentenced to twelve years' imprisonment for subversive activities. Amnestied with others in 1870, he had emigrated to the United States, and he was continuing to associate with known revolutionaries. Nature had equipped him with a ready means of disguise; shorn of his huge dark beard and with his unruly hair trimmed he became so transformed that even trackers aware of this facility could be deceived. Le Caron writes that 'in all the men I have ever met, I never saw such a change produced by so easy a process'. His conversation was so entertaining that Le Caron grew to like him, and was thus able to obtain much more information than if he had played the heavy-lidded tight-lipped sleuth.

Lomasney was to achieve notoriety in 1884 by blowing himself up while trying to fasten a bomb under London Bridge. In Detroit, however, he was merely promoting, with former fellow prisoners, the Irish Confederation, which aimed to unite the scattered and disputatious Irish in one organization. Despite the support of several leading figures, the Confederation failed to arouse mass enthusiasm. Locally unity was so markedly lacking that any newcomer allying himself with one group would have incurred the enmity of several others, so Le Caron—although anxious to penetrate the Irish republican movement in Detroit—found it prudent to stand aside. His stay in Detroit was intended to be temporary, until he had graduated, so Lomasney remained his principal source of intelligence.

Shortly after qualifying he set up his practice in Braidwood, a suburb of Wilmington, some 50 miles from Chicago. Here he continued to live the role of a Frenchman, attending with his family the Roman Catholic church, subscribing to the appropriate charities, always doing the right thing. His unpopularity did not follow him, and his supposed sympathy with the Irish republican cause brought him patients from the considerable Irish population in that mining area. In addition to his medical practice he opened a drug store; the family lived in a flat over the premises.

Soon he was appointed to the Board of Health, a sinecure carrying an annual fee of $100, and he acquired an office known as Supervisor of Braidwood, which brought him a daily fee of $2.50 and travelling allowances when engaged on town business. Concerning this appointment he comments: 'Anybody acquainted with the American political system, even to a moderate extent, will know how paying such offices can be made.' He joined his appropriate medical society, took part in founding the State Pharmaceutical Society, and campaigned for a state law regulating the practice of medicine and pharmacy.

His career as an agent might have become the minor one of contributing occasional reports on suspects but for the re-emergence of an organization founded in New York in 1867 to unite the Irish republican factions, to organize anti-English opinion and work against Anglo-American *rapprochement*. Called the Clan-na-Gael, or the United Brotherhood, its membership was confined to persons of Irish or of partial Irish descent who were supposed to be carefully selected before being admitted to its mysteries. Its branches, known as camps, were for public purposes called clubs; the first, established in New York, and named after a participant in the 1798 Irish insurrection, was entitled the Napper Tandy Club. Internally the camps were referred to by numbers. A Masonic-type form of initiation was practised with the candidate for membership (having survived an initial ballot of the members in which three black balls meant rejection) being called upon to answer questions and led blindfold into a meeting room where he was addressed on the solemnity of the oath he was about to take. Among the secrets revealed to the newly elected member were passwords and signs of recognition. At times a code was used; this was of doubtful value as it would have posed no problem to even the most amateur code-breaker, because it consisted merely of using the following letter of the alphabet—thus Ireland became Jsfmboe, and the United Brotherhood, or UB, was the VC.

As Le Caron was settling in Braidwood the Clan was experiencing a revival, putting on growth and establishing camps in the leading cities. Some of its prominent members were sufficient evidence that it was no harmless social and charitable organization. But it was not easy for him to join. He makes a fleeting reference in his auto-biography to his having been a member of the Knights of the Inner Circle, one of the bodies absorbed by the Clan, yet this membership did not give him automatic admission. His assumed nationality excluded him; as he posed as a Frenchman he could not claim to be Irish. He also had an enemy in the Clan because of his association with O'Neill and the abortive raid on Canada; this was a Major William M'Williams, a bitter opponent of the invasion leaders. Le Caron once had a fierce altercation with him when both flourished pistols and might have fired them if not separated by bystanders. Providentially M'Williams was shot dead during a row with some-one else while Le Caron was still pondering how to circumvent the opposition to his acceptance.

Eventually he was offered membership by Alexander Sullivan, whose importance was such that Le Caron's entry was unopposed. The problem of Irish descent was overcome by Le Caron's invention of Irish ancestors for his mother, and he took the Clan oath as nonchalantly as he had sworn to be loyal to the Fenian Brotherhood. He was appointed to the Military Board, a position of some status but not one which gave him a sight of secret papers or provided much information of use to Anderson and McMicken.

Documents were circulated, with a good deal of fuss about security, only to the Senior Guardians of camps, who were instructed to read them to the members and then, according to the classification, return them to headquarters or burn them in the camp's presence. All mail was kept in a strong-box with two different locks, one key being held by the Senior Guardian and the other by the Junior Guardian, so that it could not be opened by a solitary person. As an ordinary member, Le Caron could have sent his employers merely a summary from memory of the various Clan communications. His solution was to start his own camp.

The Braidwood camp which he set up was, to the public, an innocuous society—although its name commemorated a Fenian hero—called the Emmet Literary Association; inside the Clan it was Camp 463. Le Caron's election as the Senior Guardian was a matter of course; besides being the founder he was a doctor who numbered the members among his patients, a prominent citizen, and a generous contributor when the frequent subscription lists were passed round.

He still had the problem of copying the returnable papers before they went back to headquarters and of keeping the others while appearing to burn them. In his favour was the fact that people seldom adhere strictly to security regulations for long. The procedure becomes first a formality and then an annoyance; after a while it seems absurd that people who know each other well should go on checking each other's identities and observing a tiresome routine. The Junior Guardian soon ceased to insist on holding the second key, and it joined the first one on Le Caron's key-ring. Every document of importance was copied by him—a laborious task as many were very long—before it was returned.

Dealing with the material he was required to burn must have needed great coolness and at times a conjuror's skill. The average attendance at the meetings was fifteen. With this small audience so near to him he substituted other papers for the genuine ones and ostentatiously burnt them before the members. The onlookers may have been so befuddled with drink, as he alleges the Brotherhood adherents often were, as stupid as he judged them, and so poorly educated, that they saw before them only an authoritative, well-dressed man, going through a procedure whose purpose they had not wholly grasped, and whom it would be disrespectful to question.

Anderson, a specialist on Irish affairs, was kept closely informed on 'the turmoil and contention' (to borrow John Devoy's phrase), the tensions between the overt and covert organizations, the rivalries among the leaders, the periodic attempts at unity, and the relations between the movement in Ireland and in America.

Through his agent he received, among hundreds of reports, the accounts of the Skirmishing Fund, which was originally advocated in the columns of the influential *Irish World* by the jovial, hard-drinking but determined Jeremiah O'Donovan Rossa, who had been sentenced to life imprisonment for his part in the 1865 movement in Ireland and then amnestied and who was now carrying on the war against England from American soil. Five thousand dollars, he told the Irish-American readers, would have to be collected to start the campaign. Patrick Ford, the editor, commended the fund: 'What will this irregular warfare of our Irish Skirmishers effect? It will do this much. It will harass and annoy England. It will help to create her difficulty and hasten our opportunity.' In less than a year the fund grew to $23,350, without any of the expected dynamite attacks in Britain being carried out, and the subscribers became restive. To pacify them some trusted revolutionaries (including John J. Breslin, who had organized the rescue of Fenian prisoners from Australia) were invited to become trustees and the fund came effectively under the control of the Clan-na-Gael.

Breslin's prestige was, understandably, high, because the Australian adventure had been audacious, well planned and cleverly executed. The Fenians had needed a success to raise their spirits after the raid on Canada, and this exploit provided it. British Government agents, Le Caron included, appear not to have given precise warning of what was being planned; if they did, the Government failed to take effective precautions. Irishmen sentenced in Britain for subversive activities and transported to Western Australia reported, on their release and arrival in the United States, that six Fenian soldiers from the British army were still held in a penal colony near Fremantle. An Australian Prisoners Rescue Committee was formed, funds were raised to charter (on John Devoy's suggestion) a whaler, and Breslin was charged with the arrangements. A ship was commissioned at New Bedford, Massachusetts, and—to provide authenticity—a whaling crew engaged and promised some whaling on the journey. The *Catalpa*, flying the American flag, sailed on 27 April 1875, ostensibly for fishing in the South Seas. It set down its Fenian passengers while it cruised off the Australian coast. The Supreme Council of the Brotherhood of Ireland had two agents in the vicinity who aided the party from America. The prisoners, being hired out as day labourers, were easily found. Getting them on the *Catalpa* was less easy, but it was achieved, and the vessel eluded a naval craft which had been alerted when the men were discovered to be missing, and sailed out of Australian waters just in time. A dispute then arose between the crew, insisting on their right to carry out whaling, and the passengers, anxious to reach safety in the United States. The Fenians prevailed, and on 19 August 1876 they were ceremonially received in New York harbour by civic and Fenian leaders. Arguments about the financial settlement dragged on for a long time.

Encouraged by the result of this enterprise, the Fenians were in the mood for an even more daring one. Out of the Skirmishing Fund they financed the development of a submarine, a novel concept at the time, which they foresaw as a weapon for attacking British merchant ships. The inventor, then about 35, was John Philip Holland, a lay teacher in a boys' school run by the Irish Christian Brothers. He produced a small prototype and, although it sank on the first testing, it was sufficiently promising for the Skirmishing Fund trustees to put up the money for a larger version. The project could not be kept secret. Launched in 1881, it did trials in New York harbour, watched by excited crowds; one journalist called it the Fenian Ram and the name went into general use. Holland had problems of keeping it level; no suitable motive power was available; he never succeeded in devising a periscope or a projectile which could be launched from the vessel. The device became an embarrassment to the Clan; in the accounts sent by Le Caron to London it was revealed that $4,042.97 were spent on the first submarine and $23,345.70 on the second one. The Clan had not been backing a crackpot inventor—both the United States and British navies adopted Holland's ideas when they developed underwater craft—but his concepts were in advance of engineering capacity then.

Fenian imaginations ranged widely in their search for means to attack Britain. In 1876, when relations between Britain and Russia were strained, a Fenian delegation led by a Philadelphia physician, Dr William Carroll approached the Russian minister in Washington with a proposal that, in the event of war, they would fit out privateers in American ports and, carrying letters of marque from Russia, prey on British shipping; in return, Russia would assist the Irish to gain independence for Ireland. M. Shiskin, the Russian

Ambassador, did not share the view that war between his country and Britain was likely, and he explained that only in case of war could his Government negotiate with Irish revolutionaries.

In the following year another idea was mooted. An Irish force would seize Gibraltar and hold it while Spain took possession. The suggestion seems to have been put to Canovas del Castillo, the Spanish Premier, who dismissed it by referring to British naval power.

Other suggestions canvassed, and duly reported to Anderson, included the assassination of Queen Victoria and the kidnapping of the Prince of Wales or Prince Arthur. These were not seriously pursued. While Prince Arthur was in Canada serving with the Rifle Brigade and carrying out public engagements a few Fenians 'went to have a look at him', as they put it, and McMicken corresponded with Pinkerton's Agency about guarding him, but no actual threats ensued.

Anderson's standing need was information on the relationships between nationalist movements in Ireland and their counterparts in the United States. The Land League was an agrarian movement, inspired by Michael Davitt, formed in Ireland in 1879 to break landlordism. It was an overt organization, whose members were to withhold their farm rents. In practice this passive resistance led to the terrorizing of tenants who paid, or were suspected of paying, their rents, and of the landlords' agents who collected them. The word 'boycott' dates from this time; Captain Boycott, agent to Lord Erne, was subjected to treatment isolating him from the community. Persons who defied the Land League could not sell or buy in local markets; shopkeepers dared not serve them, doctors attend them, priests minister to them, undertakers bury their dead; no other child would play with their children or teachers give them instruction. Officially it belonged to the constitutional side of the Irish nationalist movement. Branches were set up in America to assist the League with funds. Through Le Caron's information the British Government knew that the American branches (which included members of the Ancient Order of Hibernians) were being taken over by the Clan-na-Gael. Clan members received secret instructions to join the Land League. Under its dutiful Senior Guardian the Braidwood camp promptly obeyed. A Land League was formed so that the Clan members could join it, and they all did.

Then two very important flies walked into the spider's parlour.

15

Gullible and Garrulous?

On New Year's Day, 1880, Charles Stewart Parnell, the leader of
the Irish party in the Westminster Parliament, and a colleague, John
Dillon, arrived in New York for a speaking tour. They visited sixty-
two towns and Parnell addressed the House of Representatives
before they hurried home for a general election in the spring. Le
Caron played no part in the tour but from secret reports and the talk
of men in the inner councils he concluded that although the ostensible
purpose was to raise funds for the overt Land League the entire trip
was managed by the covert organization. 'In the view of the conspirators scattered throughout the States,' he writes, 'Mr Parnell had
given himself over, body and soul, to the chiefs of the Clan-na-Gael.'
For all the Irish leader's professed dedication to constitutional
methods, Le Caron was convinced that he sympathized with the
men of violence. Parnell's oratory supported that view. Even the
most pacific politicians use martial imagery in discussing the clash of
principles and policies, but they run no risk of being understood
literally; on the platforms from which Parnell was speaking, however, such assertions as that, to obtain independence, 'every Irishman should be prepared to shed the last drop of his blood', were
interpreted by the audience as meaning something more vigorous
than voting in an election or moving an amendment in Parliament.

Le Caron could not, on this occasion, report directly on Parnell,
but he was able to supply Anderson with firsthand accounts of the
confidences of two leading men. The first was Michael Davitt,
released from Portland Prison on ticket of leave and now lecturing to

Land League branches. Davitt, who had lost an arm while working as a child in a Lancashire cotton mill, was a man of great ability and determination, but he was in poor health. He was avoiding, in his role as constitutionalist, any open association with the Clan-na-Gael. He visited Braidwood to address the local League; he would have had the same chairman and audience if he had talked to Camp 463 of the Clan. While there he fell ill. Dr Le Caron took him into his flat, treated him, kept him company, and listened sympathetically to his inside account of the affairs of the Land League and the whole of the Irish republican movement.

The other well-informed visitor was John Devoy, the advocate of the 'New Departure', a compact between the different forces in the Irish nationalist movement, both violent and non-violent, co-ordinating their efforts while allowing each to pursue its own path. At the age of 19, in 1861, Devoy had joined the French Foreign Legion, but he deserted to further the cause of revolution at home as a member of the Irish Republican Brotherhood. His considerable activities brought him a prison sentence; released in 1871 on condition that he left the country he went to America and worked, as did other exiles, on the New York *Herald*. His expulsion from Ireland did not prevent him from returning temporarily as a secret agent of the Clan-na-Gael. Nobody was better informed about what Anderson wanted to know.

Devoy was a dour, cantankerous man, much addicted to controversy. After being sacked from the *Herald* during a row over an Irish relief fund run by the proprietor, James Gordon Bennett, he circularized the Clan-na-Gael camps offering to lecture. A hint of his policy was contained in the sentence: 'I think the Land League has now money enough for present purposes, and that the state of things prevailing in Ireland demands that all money that can be got from our people here should be devoted to revolutionary purposes.' Le Caron seized the chance to become acquainted with Devoy and invited him to Braidwood.

A small party headed by Le Caron met him and took him to the hotel where he was booked for three or four days. On the Sunday he addressed two meetings, one of the Clan (when he allegedly forecast 'desperate work') and the other of the Land League, at both of which Le Caron presided, and he had dinner with the doctor's family in their flat. The visitor and his host had what Le Caron describes as 'many long and confidential chats', during which the meaning of that sentence in the circular letter was made plain. The money subscribed for the Land League should not all be spent on bread, Devoy argued, speaking as a member of the Revolutionary Directory of the Clan-na-Gael. As reported by Le Caron, he said: 'The organization on this side have agreed to furnish the means, and the organization in Ireland have signified their willingness to carry out a system of warfare characterized by all the rigours of Nihilism.'

Devoy confessed to a fear of a premature and therefore doomed rising in Ireland unless the fire-eating elements there could see that some action was being taken. O'Donovan Rossa, too, and his followers were forcing the pace, and had emissaries in Britain. He mentioned the names of Clan members who were preparing for active warfare, and as their talks concluded he unwittingly added something for the dossier on Parnell. Through a friend, Devoy confided, he had received a letter from Parnell stating that he was exasperated and willing to do anything. Devoy assured his host that Parnell's personal attitude to the revolutionary party was well and truly understood. What Le Caron terms 'quite an interesting budget' went to Anderson by the next mail.

Writing in the *Gaelic American* in 1923, Devoy recalled his visit to Braidwood. He denied that he had outlined a programme of 'desperate work' or given Le Caron any confidences. Referring to Le Caron's autobiography, he alleged that 'he put that stuff in to show how easily he gained the confidence of gullible and garrulous Irishmen'.

As Le Caron was so well vouched for by such a prominent man as Alexander Sullivan, Devoy need not have blamed himself for talking freely. A strict observance of security, of course, requires that even close colleagues should be told only as much as they need to know to carry out their limited part of an operation, but a rigid adherence to this principle can result in individuals failing to co-operate effectively because they do not understand the purpose of what they are doing. Senior Guardians were likely to work more usefully if they knew what kind of thinking was going on at the top. The only query in Devoy's mind concerned Le Caron's origin. He had supposed him to be of Huguenot descent or the son of a French father and an Irish mother.

'I attempted to solve the riddle of his name,' Devoy wrote forty-two years later. 'I asked him, "Where did you get your name?"

He was evidently disconcerted, thinking that I suspected him (which I did not), and replied, 'It's French.'

I said, 'I know it is, and that's why I ask you?'

'I'm a Frenchman,' he replied.

'Then how did you get into the organization?' I asked, and started to talk to him in French. This surprised him and he replied in very poor French, with an accent that was unmistakably not French. I pointed out this to him, and he explained that he had left France when a boy and was brought up in Canada among Irish people and had lost much of his native language. So he resumed talking English.

On his return to Chicago, Devoy continued, he queried Le Caron's membership with Sullivan and another Fenian leader, William J. Hynes. Hynes answered that he had never liked Le Caron and that it was Sullivan who had taken him into the organization. 'Sullivan merely said, "Le Caron is all right." I said, "But he is a Frenchman and ineligible for membership." Sullivan replied, "He fought in Canada and that makes him a good enough Irishman. Besides, I understand his mother was Irish."'

Sullivan's confidence was not shaken by Devoy's criticism of Le Caron's French, and he was soon telling him about a new campaign that would satisfy those who were complaining of the Clan's inactivity. How the attacks were to be carried out was explained by Joseph Meledy, a leading Clan member. A man named Wheeler had approached Meledy offering to supply a new type of hand grenade, so small that it could easily be carried in a 'satchel'. The Clan had acquired some and Meledy had volunteered to assist in placing them in England and Ireland.

Le Caron reported this information to London, although he did not at first appreciate its full significance.

16

A Friend from America

In the spring of 1881 Le Caron told his Fenian associates that he planned a trip to Europe for the sake of his health. His real motive was to spy on Fenian activities in Paris. The Irish Land League banked its funds there with Monroe & Company, away from British jurisdiction, and these were administered by the treasurer, Patrick Egan. John O'Leary, the liaison man between the Clan-na-Gael and the Irish Republican Brotherhood, had an office in Paris from which, assisted by John O'Connor, alias Dr Clarke or Dr Kinealy, he organized arms-smuggling into Ireland. Irish revolutionaries, some of whom had served terms in British prisons, eked out a living there in the mysterious ways that exiles do, the inevitable informers mingled with them, and occasionally detectives from London and Dublin shadowed them.

Le Caron did not pretend that he was going to take a cure at a spa; he announced that Paris was his destination. Thereupon, according to his much-disputed account, John Devoy, on behalf of the Clan-na-Gael executive, asked him to carry sealed packets to Patrick Egan and John O'Leary. There is a puzzling aspect to this story. Le Caron landed at Liverpool—the sea voyage was the only period of recuperation he had on this trip—and immediately went by train to London. He reported to Robert Anderson, showed him the packets, received a briefing, and then took them unopened to Paris. They must have been very cunningly sealed for Anderson not to use Scotland Yard's resources to open them, photograph their contents, and then reseal them. Did he consider that his agent ought not to risk the slightest suspicion of tampering?

Defending himself against later recriminations, Devoy vehemently denied that he had used Le Caron as a carrier of secret documents, and Egan agreed that he had received only a note of introduction. Here is Devoy's version, as told to an interviewer from the Chicago *Sunday Times*.

> The true story of his receiving a letter of introduction from me to Patrick Egan in Paris is this. . . . I was sitting one day in the Palmer house (Chicago) writing letters when Major Clingen, the ex-district officer and then a member of the district military board, walked into the room with Le Caron. He said that Le Caron was going to France and that the man who had succeeded him as head of the district thought it was a good opportunity to send over any important message I might not like to send by mail. I was at that time the officer in charge of such matters, but Le Caron was not supposed to know it. I told Clingen that I had a system that worked very well and that I had no message to send over. He then suggested that I should give him introductions to the heads of the organization in Ireland, but I told him that we were under pledges not to do that in the case of men going over on pleasure trips. Clingen was very disappointed and Le Caron stood by with an air of unconcern, but evidently very much interested. They went away, but returned in less than an hour and informed me that the district officer was very anxious that the doctor should have an introduction to 'somebody on the other side', and, as he himself knew nobody, he asked me as a personal favour that I should give Le Caron a letter. I then wrote on the Palmer house paper the letter which he called a 'sealed packet', but which was a mere line of introduction.

Devoy told the interviewer that he wrote two similar letters, dated 31 March 1881, in these words:

> Dear Friend: This will introduce to you a friend of mine, Dr. Le Caron of Braidwood, Ill., who is going to spend a few months in Europe. Although a Frenchman he is a member of the Land League and has always been *a good Irishman*, barring the bull. I want him to make your acquaintance and, as he treated Davitt well when in his town, I know you will show him any kindness in your power. Remembrances to all friends, Yours truly, John Devoy.

Apparently, in drafting these notes, he had forgotten his doubts about Le Caron's French origins. One letter he addressed to Egan and the other to O'Leary, and he handed them to Le Caron with the envelopes unsealed. The existence of these introductions is undisputed; the subsequent argument arose over what other papers, if any, accompanied them.

Whether what Le Caron carried were sealed packets or open introductions was unimportant compared with the chain of events started by his meeting with Egan. He was booking into the Hotel Brighton in Paris when he saw, coming down the stairs, a couple dressed for the opera. The man, good-looking, red-haired, bearded, stoutly built, was Patrick Egan. His companion was the wife of an Irish Member of Parliament and proprietor of the *Nation*, A. M. Sullivan. Le Caron merely states the fact that these two were on their way out together, and he makes no further reference to Mrs Sullivan's presence in Paris. Egan was an amiable character. After introductions he and Mrs Sullivan might well have gone on their way, with a promise to see the newcomer in the morning. Instead, he invited Le Caron to join them and immediately plunged him into the delights of a Paris which, when working there as a clerk, he could have only glimpsed from the pavements. Egan was a man living on an unaudited expense account, dining at smart restaurants and sitting in the best seats at theatres. 'He spent his money right royally,' Le Caron remarks, and comments: 'The information should be pleasant reading for the poor dupes in America and Ireland who subscribed the funds over which he was then presiding.'

As a devotee of the high life, Egan might have mistrusted this lean, sharp-featured, small man who abstained from alcohol, but he was drawn to him as O'Neill had been and gave him his confidence. In the Hotel Brighton Egan invited him to his rooms, opened his post before him and discussed the contents. They went round Paris together, talking in cabs and over restaurant and café tables, strolling in the evenings as they smoked cigars. Egan, taking advantage of the presence of a sympathizer from the United States, where much of the money came from, was anxious to explain himself.

'I am a Land Leaguer today and I shall be something else when the occasion comes,' he said. 'Meanwhile I cannot see why both organizations'—he was referring to the Land League and the Republican Brotherhood—'should not work together, the one openly, the other secretly. Parnell himself is a revolutionist to the backbone.'

Le Caron's trip was succeeding far beyond his expectations; now he felt that he was really on Parnell's trail. Encouraged to further revelations, Egan went on to tell him that Parnell had applied to join the revolutionary organization but had been rejected because it was in such chaos that the leaders thought Parnell would value it more highly if he continued to see it only from the outside.

When they discussed finance, the delicate subject of an audit was broached. Newspapers made allegations about the misuse of the substantial sums at the League's disposal, and even inside the movement suspicions were voiced about the lack of accounts. Egan said that three members of the League had examined his accounts, but any audit more public than that would give the British authorities too much information. For example, League funds had been used to finance a party of Dutch officers from Amsterdam who had gone to South Africa to help the Boers in anti-British activities. Resources had also been diverted from the League's professed purposes to help the Irish Republican Brotherhood.

O'Leary, the recipient of the other communication, lived more like a scholarly recluse, in shabby rooms at the Hôtel de la Couronne in the Latin Quarter, surrounded by books and newspapers. With a long experience as a conspirator behind him, he was at first reserved, but the two men were soon on good terms. Le Caron, the soldier, could appreciate O'Leary's dislike both of underground warfare and Parnellism and his advocacy of an open insurrectionary movement to drive the British out of Ireland. The particular object of O'Leary's contempt was John J. O'Kelly, formerly an active arms-runner, who deserted the cause by going into Parliament. Le Caron was not grudging in his assessments and he describes O'Leary as 'a fine honest fearless spirit' and 'a prince amongst his fellows of the Irish conspiracy'.

Egan's lavish hospitality lasted a fortnight. No suspicion about Le Caron's nationality arose in his mind—not surprisingly, perhaps, as Parisians are quick to understand anyone with money to spend. The pair then went to London together, where they moved convivially in Irish circles. Sullivan, the MP whose wife had accompanied Egan to the opera, invited them to dinner at his house in Clapham. They visited the Houses of Parliament, where they chatted with a group of Irish Members. Parnell joined the party.

'One of our friends from America,' Egan said, introducing his companion.

No words could have been better calculated to arouse the Irish leader's attention. He greeted Le Caron warmly and talked with him for two or three minutes. Good fellowship was expressed all round. The friend was accommodated with a seat under the gallery so that he could listen to a debate. He called again and obtained entry to the House by sending in his card to Parnell, who sent out the necessary admission. But, beyond this brief encounter, the spy had nothing to report apart from the odds and ends picked up from Parnellites. He and Egan went back to Paris separately.

His next move was determined by Parnell, who sent a message to Egan. Consequent upon this Le Caron, in a letter from Paris dated 17 May 1881, wrote to Anderson: 'Parnell writes to Egan to be sure to tell me that he wants to have a talk with me before I leave.' That potent word 'America', the source of money and therefore of power, had lodged in Parnell's brain.

Le Caron did not let the invitation grow cold. As soon as he could take his leave he rushed back to London.

On 23 May Anderson received a note from his agent that he would call on him that night after an interview with Parnell.

Arrived at the House, Le Caron sent in his card. He was not kept hanging about. To fill in the time before the leader could make himself available, O'Kelly appeared. Le Caron was well informed on this sturdy-looking character and knew that he was accused of misappropriating part of the money entrusted to him from the Skirmishing Fund, and intended to be used for gun-running, to pay his election expenses. O'Kelly took the visitor into the Members' lobby. While they were waiting for Parnell, O'Kelly asked about Le Caron's contacts in Paris, and spoke his mind about O'Leary.

'An old fossil!' he exclaimed.

Le Caron fuelled O'Kelly's wrath by revealing O'Leary's view that he had betrayed the cause by going into Parliament. While among the parliamentarians, Le Caron was willing to agree with whatever opinions they expressed.

What was on O'Kelly's mind was the state of the movement in Ireland, where the secret organization, the Irish Republican Brotherhood, was still opposing the Land League. O'Kelly was urging that the leaders in America should put pressure on the Irish to work in unison when Le Caron felt a tap on his shoulder.

'I want to see you.'

The tall Parnell looked down at him. His eyes were sad. He gestured towards the library corridor. The three moved, taking the route which passes behind the Speaker's chair. O'Kelly took his leave.

Members were continually going by, but the spy and the uncrowned king of Ireland were virtually alone together. Detectives watched them as, for three-quarters of an hour, they sedately paced the corridors. At that time a state bordering on civil war existed in some parts of Ireland; 30,000 soldiers and 12,000 policemen were engaged there. Scotland Yard was interested in the Irish Members' contacts and Anderson, forewarned by Le Caron's note, would have ensured that Parnell was kept under observation that evening.

Leaning towards his visitor, Parnell spoke in low tones. Other conversations were proceeding around them. The detectives could hear nothing of what either man said. Le Caron's is the only version of what transpired.

O'Kelly's conversation had prepared Le Caron for what was uppermost in the leader's mind—the tensions between the secret and the open movements in Ireland. If the American organization withheld material assistance, Parnell suggested, the Irish would have to fall into line.

'You furnish the sinews of war,' Le Caron recollected him saying, 'and if they do not do as you tell them, stop the supplies. The whole matter rests in your hands.'

Parnell believed that Devoy could do more than anyone else to bring about a clear understanding and alliance. He charged Le Caron to see Devoy immediately on his return to New York and to invite him, at Parnell's expense, to meet him in Paris. Le Caron was then to see other prominent Fenians—Alexander Sullivan, William J. Hynes and Dr William Carroll—explain Parnell's attitude, and ask either Sullivan or Hynes to cross the Atlantic for a discussion. No misunderstanding need arise, Parnell said, as they were all working for a common purpose, the independence of Ireland. Then the parliamentary leader made an admission which Le Caron describes as 'a veritable bombshell'.

'Doctor, I have long since ceased to believe that anything but the force of arms will ever bring about the redemption of Ireland.'

In a manner 'grave and impassive', with 'no uncertainty, no indistinctness in his utterance', Parnell went on to consider the practical aspects of revolution: the resources required for an open insurrectionary movement, the men and money to be raised, what American assistance would be needed. By the end of the year, he revealed, the Land League treasury would have £100,000 available.

'You fellows ought to do as well as that,' he remarked.

Complaisant as he always was when gathering intelligence, Le Caron undertook to do everything that Parnell had requested.

Perhaps it was to throw off followers that Le Caron then took a seat under the gallery to listen to the proceedings. In his autobiography he fails to recollect correctly the subject before the House that evening, but his mind must have been full of what he had just heard. To have secured this private interview with Parnell was his greatest coup since the Fenian invasion of Canada in 1870.

It was late when he emerged into Parliament Square. A dapper, top-hatted figure, very like the other gentlemen entering and leaving the building, and no doubt with a slight swagger of triumph, he would have paused outside to light a cigar. A hansom left the rank as he raised a hand.

'Thirty-nine, Linden Gardens, Bayswater,' he ordered. Nobody followed him.

While Anderson wrote at his desk, recording what he later called 'this historic interview', Le Caron talked and smoked cigars.

Dawn was breaking when he rose to go. He was very tired, but his brain was working clearly. If Anderson passed this report on, he was thinking, and any part of it got into unsympathetic hands, the informant could be easily identified. The consequence would be his own murder.

At the door he paused, and said in what Anderson termed his customary cynical manner:

'Now, if you want to get rid of me, here is your chance!'

To suppress a report of this importance was unthinkable, but Anderson shared Le Caron's thoughts. How to exploit secret information without compromising the source is the ever-recurrent problem in intelligence work. He kept the story to himself until he heard that his agent had arrived home, and then he passed it on as 'received from an American informant'.

17

Dynamite in the Air

In the tea room of the House of Commons, Parnell was entertaining a visitor, a smartly dressed, sharp-featured man who had previously been seen in the Member's company. Just before they said a cordial goodbye, Parnell handed over a photograph of himself, the kind he distributed to particularly favoured admirers. 'Yours very truly Chas. S. Parnell' was written in the bottom margin. The recipient was to treasure this gift, although not for a reason that the donor would have guessed. It was, for Le Caron, a certificate that he had met and talked with Parnell.

Dublin was to be his next place of call. At a briefing by Anderson, he displayed his credentials: letters of introduction to Egan's brother-in-law, O'Rorke; to Dr J. E. Kenny MP; and to the Land League headquarters in Sackville Street. No spy could have been better equipped to walk unquestioned into the enemy's camp.

With Dr Kenny as his host, all doors were open to him—including the heavy studded portal of Kilmainham Prison, where several prominent Nationalists were detained under the 'Suspects Act'. Prison rules stipulated that meetings between inmates and visitors must be supervised and no papers passed between them without permission, but these regulations were openly flouted; either the prison staff were sympathizers or they were intimidated. As soon as Le Caron settled down to talk to Michael Boyton, the man in charge of the 'active policy', the warder moved out of earshot. Boyton, a paid organizer of the League, assured the visitor that the open movement had stimulated the revolutionary one, and now they required arms, organization and leaders; he had a claim to United States citizenship which, if established, would help his release, and he gave a letter and photograph into Dr Kenny's care for Le Caron to take back with him.

As if to reinforce his credibility, while Le Caron was calling on prominent Nationalists, and visiting Mr Sexton, the Lord Mayor of Dublin, an envelope posted in the House of Commons arrived for him at the Land League containing another signed photograph of Parnell.

O'Rorke and some associates accompanied him to the ship on his departure and stood talking with him until visitors were warned to go ashore. Men who were constantly reminding their followers to beware of spies and traitors waved to him as the vessel moved away. To Anderson he reported on his conversations and the state of affairs in Kilmainham Prison. 'I was commended for my success,' he writes.

He landed in New York on 12 June 1881. In view of later assertions that Parnell never gave him any instructions, it is important to note that immediately on arriving he endeavoured to carry out what he claimed were the Irish leader's requests and that the persons concerned responded in the belief that the messages were genuine. Devoy was in New Haven, Connecticut, so Le Caron, who had hoped to see him in New York, sent him a telegram before going home to Braidwood.

In his absence he had put on weight, a fact which supported the pretext of having taken the trip for his health. Despite his healthier appearance, however, he was tired from his activities while away and from the journey, yet he could give himself no respite. Matters concerning his medical practice and pharmacy business awaited his attention, and circulars had accumulated for the Senior Guardian of the Braidwood camp,, among them one from the Clan-na-Gael headquarters dated 1 March soliciting contributions towards military preparations. The line was familiar. The leaders were trying simultaneously to stir up enthusiasm and damp down impatience: under the heading 'A few words of counsel and warning', members were informed that 'the hour to strike has not yet arrived'. The text confirmed what Le Caron had told Anderson, that while the Clan had not as an organization gone into the Land League, individual members had. Its conclusion was that the time was fast approaching when the two bodies must act together.

On receiving a telegram from Devoy Le Caron wrote from Braidwood on 18 June.

> My dear Devoy,—Your telegram received—I have just time by this mail to write you but one item that I have been requested to convey to you. Your friend Mr. E. [Egan], desires, though the request comes through me to you direct from Mr. P. [Parnell], that you at the earliest practicable moment meet them in Paris.
>
> Mr. P. desired me to assure you that there would be no trouble upon the head of your personal expense. He would see that you would be properly reimbursed. Doubting the prudence of writing you *full* details, I will by next mail send you general outlines of what they desire.
>
> Doubtless you have heard ere this from Mr. E. upon this subject. The night before leaving I had a long interview with Mr. P. upon this subject and permit me to say that knowing the reliance and confidence placed in you by him I think that by acceding to his wishes you would accomplish much good.—Fraternally yours, H. Le Caron.

Under the same date Le Caron wrote a longer letter, rather confused and with some slips of the pen revealing his fatigue. He hinted at instead of explaining explicitly what Parnell had said.

> Through your courtesy I found Mr. E. of Paris a noble hearted jolly good companion, and in going to London in his company I came in contact with your friend Mr. P. upon several occasions. Their views upon the national question I should infer from what was said you are well acquainted with. I found upon their part a knowledge of the necessity of an understanding and a determination to if possible bring about a unity of purpose. Circumstances have continually occurred showing them the necessity. . . .
>
> His programme in detail for the future though more in detail was almost identical with that of Mr. E. He desired that I should convey to you his ideas, intentions and desires, and I think they are upon a basis that you and every liberty-loving revolutionist can agree upon hence as I have written you his desire to see you. W.J.H. [W. J. Hynes] has promised to write you.
>
> If I am not sufficiently plain write me for the items of detail you require. I had a very enjoyable time and came back well, with a gain of twenty-two pounds of adipose tissue.—Yours truly, H. Le Caron.

Devoy's reply acknowledged the message from Parnell. He wrote on 24 June from the premises of James Reynolds, brass founder, New Haven (where the 'Fenian Ram' had come to rest), addressing Le Caron as 'Dear Friend'. Part of his letter read:

> I am much obliged for the information you give me, and the interest you have taken in a matter that affects us all so closely. I have not heard from H. [W. J. Hynes] yet. Yesterday I received a short note from E., urging me strongly to go over, but I did not understand for what purpose till I got your explanation. I would like to go very much if I could spare the time, and if I thought my visit would produce the effect anticipated, but I am afraid it would not. . . . All I could do would be to tell E. and P. on my own responsibility, what I believed would satisfy our friends here, and make propositions that I might feel morally certain would be approved of. But I would not on any consideration have them pay my expenses. That would place me in a false position at once.

Carrying out Parnell's requests Le Caron met or wrote to other Clan-na-Gael leaders. Sullivan was gratified but suggested that action should be postponed until the August Convention in Chicago but the leaders were not unanimous about an alliance. In particular, William Carroll, a Philadelphia doctor and a power in the Clan, 'appeared anything but an enthusiast on Mr Parnell's behalf, although in the end he went the length of saying that he was glad to find by Mr Parnell's attitude that there was a returning sense of reason on his part'.

It was evident that the forthcoming secret Convention in Chicago would be of exceptional importance. His dealings with McMicken had in recent years been only intermittent but now he resumed correspondence with him. Nearly 68, McMicken had retired from his post as Chief Commissioner of Police and was managing the Manitoba and North West Agency in Winnipeg of the Commercial Union Assurance Company. He wrote to Sir John Macdonald conveying Le Caron's information and commenting: 'He is evidently in an important and trusted position amongst them. In former times he proved himself to be most reliable, trustworthy and serviceable. I believe him so still. . . . He has now a family of 6 children, and being an M.D. absence injures his means of living from it.'

Suggesting that Le Caron should be paid $100 a month, with a promise as before of a sum if his services proved of value, McMicken reminded Sir John of the agent's original stipulation to which he still adhered: 'He will only address himself to me.' McMicken proposed that he should control the arrangement while one of his sons in the police service would do the detailed work.

Three weeks after writing that letter, McMicken received from Le Caron the Clan executive's report, showing 14,000 members and funds of $100,000. To supplement the inside information they would get, the police department detailed detectives who would penetrate the hall if possible and circulate among the delegates in the bars.

Newspapermen had received hints that this Convention, from which all outsiders were to be excluded, would provide sensational material. Competition among reporters was fierce. Before the proceedings opened on 3 August upper rooms in the building had been rented and a discreet hole bored through the ceiling above the chairman's seat. Accommodation in houses across the street had been booked, from which pressmen with binoculars could peer into the hall. Delegates were buttonholed in bars and plied, not unwillingly, with drinks. Editors employed men from two detective agencies—Pinkerton's and Tuttle's—to use whatever techniques they needed to get in the hall or to persuade delegates to talk. Reporters posed as delegates, messengers, attendants, adopting any ruse to slip past the guards.

Against this onslaught, the Convention managers organized an impressive security procedure. They posted sentries who were large, muscular and of forbidding appearance. Before approaching the meeting room participants, known by numbers instead of names, had to present their credentials; after these were checked, they were given a whispered password. They moved into a corridor leading to the place of assembly, where their passage was barred by more strong-arm men who again looked at their papers and demanded to hear the password. These guards then mouthed another word—the inside password—and this had to be repeated to the two attendants who stood at the closed door behind which the meeting was taking place. The door was then opened and the legitimate delegates, who included Le Caron, were free to enter. Whether this drill was scrupulously followed throughout the following sessions is doubtful. It is easy to imagine the impatience of jostling delegates, and the boredom of guards, going through this routine time after time. It is easy to imagine, too, the inducements to delegates to rent out their admission papers and the lavish tips offered. Amused at these futile precautions, Le Caron remarks: 'Like all proceedings from which the general public are shut out, a Clan-na-Gael assembly becomes interesting in proportion to the amount of secrecy by which it is attended.'

Le Caron seldom abandons his pedestrian style for a descriptive passage, but the 1881 Convention provided a scene he felt moved to describe. It is, he comments, 'very Irish—very Irish indeed'.

> What a sight! What a babel of voices and a world of smoke! You can scarce see for the clouds which curl and roll round you as the breath of fresh air is admitted by the opening door, while, as for hearing, your ears are deafened by the din and clatter of many tongues and stamping feet. Yes, we are at last in the Irish Parliament, as it is grandly termed, in full session. . . . It partakes, on the first view, more of the character of 'free and easy' entertainment than a grave portentous gathering of conspirators; but you must not judge by first appearances or outward characteristics. It is the way these men have of doing their business, and the dread character of their work is in no way affected by the almost ludicrous phases of the preliminary performance. Always you must remember that you are dealing with Irishmen, who in their wildest and most ferocious of fights still retain that substratum of childishness of character and playfulness of mood, with its attendant elements of exaggeration and romance, which make it as difficult for an ordinary House of Commons member to rightly understand his Irish colleague when he launches forth in description or invective, as it is for the civilized foreigner to know where the actual grievance now comes in. . . . They are a funny crowd, as lolling with arms akimbo, and thumbs resting in their waistcoat arm-holes, they hang their feet on the chairs in front, which for comfort's sake are tilted to an angle of some 40 or 45 degrees, and puff their cigars—on such an occasion there is nothing so vulgar as a pipe indulged in—high up into the air, changing their position now and again in order to have a pull at those interesting-looking black bottles, or to disrobe themselves of coat or waistcoat, the better to cool their heated frames.

Fights broke out every hour, Le Caron reports, but the proceedings were only briefly interrupted, as in less than a quarter of an hour the combatants would be amicably drinking out of the same bottle. Verbal violence was also frequent. Le Caron observes that 'all are engaged in applauding revolutionary sentiment spiced with religious quotation'. One popular speaker was T. V. Powderly, chief of 'The Knights of Labour', who made this declaration:

> The killing of English robbers and tyrants in Ireland, and the destruction by any and all means of their capital and resources, which enables them to carry on their robberies and tyrannies, is not a needless act. Hence I am in favour of the torch for their cities and the knife for their tyrants till they agree to let Ireland severely alone. London, Liverpool, Manchester, and Bristol in ashes may bring them to view it in another light.

Violence to further 'the holy work in which we are engaged' (to quote the president, James Reynolds) was the theme of the Convention. Engineering, chemicals and mining, described as branches of warfare suitable to the age, were to be studied by a committee, and a course of instruction was announced. Undeterred by the expense incurred on the submarines, delegates considered a proposal to equip a cruiser to damage the enemy's commerce and colonies, and some were enthusiastic about a suggested expedition to South America to attack 'a little place' illegally occupied by the English. The rescue of Michael Davitt (on whose defence $1,532 had been spent) from Portland Prison was mooted but reluctantly dismissed as impracticable. The past expenditure of $10,000 on 'tools' (weapons) for Ireland was approved. One idea, which caused no rush of volunteers, was that loyal Fenians should join the British navy with the intention of attaching dynamite to lumps of coal in ships' bunkers, so that at any time a stoker's shovelful could blow the vessel to pieces.

The most prominent advocate of terrorism, O'Donovan Rossa, who had constantly attacked the Clan as too gradualist, had a one-line mention in the accounts: 'O'Donovan Rossa's defalcations, $1,321.90.' A neighbouring item read: 'Stolen by messenger of *Irish World*, $27.50.' The messenger's reputation may have been damaged, but in the long run Rossa's was not, and he remained a hero of the revolutionary movement. Like O'Neill before the invasion of Canada, the Executive had to defend itself against criticisms of

inaction by adopting a pose no less fierce than that of its critics while
determined to go at its own pace. At this Convention the leaders,
while not disdaining the customary rhetoric in the main hall,
refrained from committing themselves to naval or military adven-
tures but actively supported projects explored, in practical detail, by
small groups of conspirators in side rooms.

Chain-smoking but sober, Le Caron moved freely among the
delegates. He talked to the affable William Mackey Lomasney, one
of the men certain to be sent to England to place bombs in public
places, and to another future dynamitard, the dapper Dr Thomas
Gallagher. He renewed his acquaintance with John O'Connor,
whom he had met in Paris when calling on O'Leary. O'Connor was
there as an envoy of the Supreme Council of the Irish Republican
Brotherhood in Ireland, charged to ensure that American financial
support did not diminish because of fears that the Irish Fenians were
influenced by the insufficiently revolutionary Land League. What
he heard at the Convention had reassured him, and he told Le Caron
that he thought his home organization and the Clan understood each
other well enough. As O'Connor was kept in seclusion, and did not
appear before committees, Le Caron's access to him showed how
completely he was trusted as an insider.

Although the claim to be the 'Irish Parliament' was a mere
propaganda one—the bulk of the Irish population in America displayed little active interest—this Convention was representative of
the Clan-na-Gael at all levels. The Irish who had done well were in
evidence: forty lawyers, eight doctors, two judges, clergymen,
merchants and manufacturers were present. The bulk, of course,
were working men. In the hall they were (to quote Le Caron again)
'almost all mixed up in glorious confusion, almost all reduced to the
level of the whisky bottle, and none removed from the struggles of
personal avarice and ambition'.

John Devoy, in his reminiscences in the *Gaelic American* in 1923,
gave a different account of this and other Conventions.

> The spy's descriptions of Clan Conventions are grotesque in their
> falsehood except in the matter of smoking—and in that he only
> thickens the smoke to the extent of almost wholly darkening the
> hall. He places two or three bottles of whisky on the table, sends
> the delegates up to take a swig now and then and starts fierce fights,

uproarious shouting and all kinds of disorder, so that no real business can be done. This suited the English idea of Irish conventions and he was catering to the tastes of his own countrymen. I have been attending Clan-na-Gael conventions for fifty years and I never saw a bottle of whisky at any of them. Whatever drinking was done took place in hotel bars, and drunkenness was a very rare occurrence. Men who have had long experience of political and society gatherings describe the Clan-na-Gael meetings as models of good order and decorum and the average of intelligence as of a very high order. The debates are always well conducted and there are always a few men of very superior ability among the delegates.

Drunk or sober, brawlers or models of decorum, the delegates followed a clear trend. They elected as president the ruthless Alexander Sullivan, termed by Le Caron 'the arch plotter' and now practising as a lawyer, while increasing the president's powers. They reduced the Executive (referred to as the FC of the VC) to six for greater effectiveness. A resolution affirmed that they did not endorse the idea of dynamite but were willing to use even that against 'the army of occupation'.

Le Caron warned Anderson that dynamite was 'in the air'.

In November of the same year Le Caron was instructed by the 'VC' to attend the forthcoming Irish National Convention in Chicago and to ensure that members of his camp attended as delegates of whatever Irish society existed in the neighbourhood. Thus members of the secret Clan-na-Gael were to be present representing the Land League or even the Ancient Order of Hibernians (a friendly society whose branches had largely affiliated with the overt Land League).

The plan worked smoothly. Before the Convention opened the Clan-na-Gael members were briefed secretly as to how they were to vote on resolutions and which committee candidates to support. The resolutions to be adopted in the open conference were drafted by the Clan-na-Gael caucus. A prominent member, John F. Finerty of Chicago, was nominated to make the opening speech; he in turn appointed William J. Hynes as temporary presiding officer; two of their number, Ronan and Powderly (who had at the August Convention urged the killing of English robbers and tyrants in Ireland), were made temporary secretaries. The Revd. Dr G. C. Betts, a pro-dynamite Episcopalian clergyman, was appointed permanent chairman, despite the opposition of less militant clerics known as the Moral Suasion Faction. The Clan's domination was complete.

At that time Parnell was still detained in Kilmainham Prison, but two members of his party at Westminster, T. P. O'Connor and T. Healy, attended. A reception was held for them. Their speeches were intended to assure American activists that Irish politicians were no less passionately anti-British than they themselves, even though their methods differed. Mr Healy declared that 'the land system of Ireland is the nerve centre, is the ganglion, is the heart of British rule, and I believe that if you want to break the British rule you must strike it through the land system and landlordism.' He was speaking six weeks after the Land League in Ireland had been suppressed. It looked as though the British Government, in detaining the politicians and closing down the Land League, was convinced that the parliamentary movement and the men of violence were in league, but Le Caron continued his work with the same ceaseless energy that he had devoted to bringing down O'Neill.

Anyone observing him would have seen only an ordinary reliable delegate, an unobtrusive conformist always voting with the majority. Profiting by his experience of coming under suspicion, he made no notes during the gatherings, but he had an exceptionally good memory and he avidly collected circulars and newspaper cuttings. While other delegates were lounging in the bars until the small hours, he was sitting alone, writing page after page, kept awake by his determination and a succession of cigars.

Such regular and extensive reports gave Anderson an advantage over his colleagues and aroused their jealousy. One of them picked up the name Thomas—Le Caron wrote in the name of Thomas Beach—and, assuming it to be a surname, sent a detective to Chicago to discover the source. The mission failed, but in 1882 the agent's name was passed between offices in an alarming manner.

Archibald, the New York Consul, then aged 72, was postponing his retirement until the partly run-down British Intelligence network in America could be reorganized. Whitehall sent the 62-year-old Sir John Rose to study the situation. Born in Scotland, Rose had at 16 been taken to Canada by his parents, where he had a distinguished career as a lawyer and statesman. Later he settled in London and, regarded as an authority on Canadian and United States affairs, occasionally undertook missions for the British Government. During his tour he called on McMicken, from whom—surprisingly—he received Le Caron's name, Post Office box number in Braidwood, and an assurance of this agent's reliability. When Rose reported personally in London to Sir William Harcourt, Home Secretary and minister responsible for the Secret Service, Anderson was called into consultation. As Le Caron's name had been concealed even from his superior, James Monro, it must have startled Anderson to learn that Rose had inquired about Le Caron in New York, where McMicken's commendation had been endorsed. Questioned by Harcourt, Anderson claimed to know the Braidwood doctor very well and volunteered information about him. Anderson never explained why he was so forthcoming at this meeting; he may have hoped to impress the minister, now that the much-guarded name had been revealed. But he stood his ground, when asked whether the contact might join the projected network, by asserting that Le Caron would regard as an insult a proposal that he should report to the police or a government office. The right course, Anderson suggested, would be to refer the matter back to Judge McMicken.

When the Judge appeared in Chicago to put the proposition to him that he should join a new set-up, Le Caron thought his visitor was acting under strong pressure from London. He seems not to have suspected that McMicken had volunteered his name in the first place or to have learned that Archibald knew about him. McMicken appears to have acted somewhat out of character here but, to do him justice, he may not have known of Le Caron's continuing and exclusive contract with Anderson or to have seen any reason not to talk frankly to such a trusted emissary as Rose. As Anderson had anticipated, Le Caron rejected the suggestion out of hand. Later Anderson commented: 'If Le Caron had yielded to the overtures then made to him he might have named his own terms.'

Rose's report, 'Secret Consular Agencies in the United States', dated 13 September 1882, and circulated internally, contained Le Caron's name and postal address. Reports often move with great rapidity from In to Out trays, and it is possible that nobody on the distribution list studied this one sufficiently to guess that Thomas and Le Caron were identical. A chink in the security barrier surrounding Le Caron had been revealed but his usual luck held. Archibald, the other man who knew something about him, died two years later.

Whether, if he had named his own terms, Le Caron would have got the money is doubtful. Rose's plan was shelved, partly on the grounds of expense.

18

A Warning to Informers

Around the time when the Clan was so ably manipulating the American Land Leaguers and Hibernians at the Convention, an independent group of about thirty would-be assassins, calling themselves the Invincibles, was forming in Ireland.

In Chicago the implementation of plans made at the 1881 Clan-na-Gael Convention proceeded. By early 1882 a bomb school offered courses run by the organization's explosives expert, Dr Patrick Cronin, whom Le Caron knew not only as a Clan member but as a fellow medical man. A keen student of chemistry, Dr Thomas Gallagher, aged 31, was appointed to reconnoitre London. Fashionably dressed, carrying a gold-headed cane, he paced the ship's deck, courteously greeting other passengers, the model of a well-to-do gentleman. Sullivan's instructions to him were to keep away from all Irish groups and even to avoid Irish Members of Parliament. Gallagher surveyed the London main stations and the underground railway, prospected Scotland Yard, visited the Tower as any tourist might, and got himself invited to the House of Commons, where he was introduced to Gladstone.

In April an appeal by the Clan to all officers and men to join rifle clubs and take part in a few days' field service marked the start of a campaign to strengthen the Revolutionary Directory (referred to as the RD), a highly secret body whose names were known only to the Clan Executive in America and the Supreme Council of the Irish Republican Brotherhood in the United Kingdom. The first circular was followed by the customary request for contributions and the suggestion that all able-bodied men should join the state militia to acquire a military training.

The British Cabinet had debated for five hours before agreeing to arrest Parnell, and they were ready to respond when he made a conciliatory move. Captain O'Shea, one of Parnell's parliamentary team, acted as his emissary to assure Gladstone that the Irish leader wished to use his influence on behalf of peace. The Kilmainham Treaty was signed on 2 May 1882, Parnell pledging himself to support Gladstone in forwarding Liberal principles and Gladstone undertaking to promote what the Land League would regard as a practical settlement of the land question.

The hoped-for period of tranquillity did not follow. On 6 May the Invincibles struck. Lord Frederick Cavendish, the Chief Secretary to the Lord-Lieutenant, and Mr Thomas Henry Burke, the Under-Secretary, were walking together through Phoenix Park, Dublin, when they were stabbed to death by men wielding long surgical knives. When Parnell, now at liberty, heard the news he appeared badly shaken; he at once denounced the crime, and declared that it was a setback to the Irish cause.

Le Caron had no information about the Invincibles and the incident (except for the reactions to it inside the Clan and the arrival in the United States of men who found it prudent to get away quickly) was outside the scope of his reporting, but it started a chain of events which increasingly involved him and determined his career. If the regular Dublin correspondent of *The Times* had covered the trial of the assassins Le Caron might have remained an obscure character traceable only through Judge McMicken's files. It happened, however, that the proceedings were reported by a very young Irish journalist, Edward Caulfield Houston. He sat throughout the trial, during which evidence for the prosecution was given by one of the Invincibles named James Carey, and he came away feeling that he had a mission. Convinced of an association between Irish parliamentarians and the perpetrators of the Phoenix Park murders and other outrages, he set out on his own initiative to get the full story. In the course of his researches he became secretary of an anti-Home Rule society calling itself the Irish Loyal and Patriotic Union.

To prepare a base for Gallagher's operations, a bomb school graduate, James Murphy, in February 1883 rented a shop in Ledsam Street,

Ladywood, Birmingham, posing as a retailer of paint and wallpaper. While waiting for the team to assemble, he collected materials for the manufacture of nitroglycerine.

At the same time the team's sponsors were recruiting reinforcements for bombing parties and apparently planning to raise an armed force. Senior Guardians of camps received a circular from the Revolutionary Directory asking them to furnish the names and addresses of 'men best fitted for private work of a confidential and dangerous character' and suggesting that military organizations should be set up covering all branches of land and marine warfare. Picnics, balls and entertainments were to be promoted to raise funds. Doubtful and suspicious members were to be reported and watched. Members were to give the National League all possible support. This circular was succeeded by another emphasizing the importance of securing a full attendance at the forthcoming national convention.

News soon came that the initial investment in the current terrorist campaign had been lost. On 5 April before they could stage a single explosion, Dr Gallagher and his men were arrested.

Le Caron attended the convention in Philadelphia on 25 April in the dual capacity of delegate from the Robert Emmet Club (the Braidwood camp) and the local Land League. As at the previous national meeting, secret caucuses held preliminary meetings and arranged every detail of the agenda. The Land League formally ceased to exist—despite the efforts of priests and women members to keep it going—and was retitled the National League of America. As planned, Alexander Sullivan was appointed president after two well-staged refusals to be nominated, and five out of seven of the executive committee were Clan-na-Gael members. The procurer of the knives used in the Phoenix Park murders, Frank Byrne, was present with his wife, who had conveyed these implements to the killers; the couple's arrival in America had been financed by Egan, and now they were circulating among the delegates. A chairman's post was refused to Mr P. A. Collins of Boston because he had publicly offered a reward for the arrest of the Phoenix Park murderers.

A telegram from Parnell in London, discreetly worded but well understood by the executive, was read, of which this was the main passage:

I would respectfully advise that your platform be so framed as to enable us to continue to accept help from America, and at the same time avoid offering a pretext to the British Government for entirely suppressing the national movement in Ireland. In this way only can unity of movement be preserved both in Ireland and America. I have perfect confidence that by prudence, moderation, and firmness the cause of Ireland will continue to advance, and though persecution rests heavily upon us at present, before many years have passed we shall have achieved those great objects for which through many centuries our race has struggled.

Egan, one of the men the British police were seeking following the Phoenix Park murders, had received a tip-off from a contact in Dublin Castle that a warrant for his arrest had been issued. Within twenty minutes he was destroying letters from Carey and documents relating to the Irish Republican Brotherhood, and packing clothes, while a friend was buying him a ticket to Belfast. From there, via Manchester, Hull, Rotterdam and Paris, he had reached America. He was now attending the open meetings of the convention, where he revealed that of the $1,230,000 funds he had received, $1 million came from America. As he thought it inadvisable to attend the secret meetings, he relied on Le Caron for accounts of what was going on behind the scenes. In return he gave Le Caron his confidence, assuring him that an understanding had been reached and that the future programme would be satisfactory to all nationalists.

The executive, highly gratified by the result of the convention, conveyed its jubilation to the camps in a secret circular dated 12 May: 'Brothers, we most heartily congratulate you and the cause upon the splendid discipline and the perfect harmony at the recent public gathering.' Instructions followed on how to keep secret the fact that the Clan was running the organization. The names of the Senior and Junior Guardians must be concealed from the public organization, but brothers who were not officers could be designated as president and secretary and allowed to conduct correspondence with the League. Members who suspected that the Clan was going soft in this collaboration with the open movement were assured that the Revolutionary Directory was organizing 'most important measures'.

Le Caron had two reports to prepare, one for Anderson and one for his camp. Anderson received a set of the papers issued at the Convention, with the accounts and the substance of Le Caron's conversations with Sullivan, Egan and other key men. To his camp he gave a delegate's conventional report of the proceedings, concluding with an inordinately long sentence in a style which could scarcely have been bettered by a genuine Irish Fenian.

> To briefly summarize the results of the Convention, we find the unification of all Irish societies pledged under one leadership to follow the lines laid down by Parnell and the party at home, not to lead but to follow them whence they may go with all the energy, practical and financial support possible—a proof to the world that the ten millions of Irish nationality upon the continent can be represented in convention by their 1,200 delegates, and work harmoniously and unitedly, and giving to those, and their number is legion, who believe in force alone, the supreme satisfaction of knowing that the machinery of the cause is now under the control and direction of their comrades, who believe, as they do, that dynamite, or any other species of warfare that can be devised is perfectly legitimate, so long as it can be made effective, and accomplish results permanent and tangible.

During a train journey from Chicago to Milwaukee in May, when they were travelling to a demonstration in honour of Egan, Le Caron tried to learn more of the bombing campaign from Sullivan. On returning from his exploratory trip to London, Gallagher had spoken enthusiastically to Le Caron about the suitability as targets of London public buildings but the detailed plans were known only to the participants. Although he had approved the expedition, Sullivan was as much in the dark as Le Caron as to what had happened. Sullivan had convinced himself that Gallagher's capture was due to the treachery of the Clan's competitor, O'Donovan Rossa and his Skirmishers. Gallagher, Sullivan declared, had disregarded his order not to associate with Rossa's men, who had betrayed his plans to a paid informer, Jim McDermott. What Sullivan did not know was that Gallagher had an understanding with Rossa, who was happy that the Clan should bear the expense. Rossa had not in fact betrayed an operation in which he had an interest.

Gallagher could not risk bringing dynamite through the controls at the British ports, so he decided to manufacture it in England.

Birmingham was chosen as a suitable place because of its large Irish population. Murphy aroused suspicion not because he was Irish but because a storeman employed by wholesale chemists wondered why a small shopkeeper should be buying such large quantities of pure glycerine. He told the police, who surreptitiously searched the premises, trailed Murphy and waited until they could pounce on the entire gang. One of them turned Queen's evidence, thus introducing a traitor to the story, but he added little to what the prosecution already knew.

In future, the angry Sullivan told his sympathetic companion, he would select for training only men who would not exceed their instructions, who had no families and—a point Le Caron noted with amusement—whose backgrounds had been exhaustively investigated. Before the train reached Milwaukee Sullivan had claimed to have information from Ireland that forty Royal Irish Constabulary men had been sent to America on full pay; if true, this meant that Clan contacts were inside the most secret departments in Dublin. He had also explained the organization, methods and finances of the Revolutionary Directory. From this conversation Le Caron gained enough material for a thesis.

Egan had succeeded in his mission of persuading the American-Irish that the constitutional movement on the other side remained firm in its revolutionary aims. The Irish National League of America signalled that all was well by sending greeting to its honoured and esteemed leader, Charles Stewart Parnell, pledging its hearty support of the platform and policy adopted by the Irish National League in Dublin, and promising to be in the future, as in the past, true to its patriotic leaders. The Clan promoted a 'Parnell testimonial', headed by Alexander Sullivan's signature, calling on camps to raise money to support those Irish Members of Parliament who had no other means of income—British Members of Parliament at that time received no salaries.

That summer the Fenian movement rejoiced over a revenge. On 29 July 1883, James Carey, the informer who had betrayed the Invincibles after the Phoenix Park murders, was shot dead by Patrick O'Donnell, a Donegal man. The impact of this revenge killing was enormously heightened by where it took place. So far as the public knew, Carey had disappeared; he had in fact gone a long way. As Patrick Ford, the editor of the *Irish World* put it: 'Carey, the traitor-informer, taking shelter under the wings of the British Empire, had skulked away to parts unknown.' He was on board the steamship *Melrose*, between Capetown and Natal, when he was murdered. O'Donnell could not have expected to avoid arrest, but he hoped that, after his seizure on board and during his five weeks' detention on shore in Africa, he would be snatched away. Rumours circulated that the Clan was mounting a rescue. The Fenians had demonstrated, through the agency of O'Donnell, that their arm was long, but it failed to pick up O'Donnell himself. He was shipped back to England for trial. The *Irish World* promoted an O'Donnell Defence Fund and raised $65,000 for legal costs and for compensation for the families of the executed Phoenix Park assassins (the family of one man was excluded from these benefits because he expressed contrition and pleaded guilty).

The warning implicit in Carey's fate was underlined in a secret circular sent out in September, read by Le Caron to the Braidwood camp and copied for Anderson. It made the best of Gallagher's venture which had ended in sentences of life imprisonment:

> Though the efforts of your Executive have not been fully realized, or rather were marred by the informer's treason, yet those brothers (with one solitary exception) entrusted with the work did nobly, and were at the very threshold of deeds that would have startled the world, and put the fear of the organization in the hearts of the enemy. These brothers have with heroic faith carried your secrets to the dungeon under a fate and torture worse than death. They did nobly. It was by no fault of theirs they failed.

Then came a statement of policy:

> We cannot see our way for an armed insurrection in Ireland this side of some great foreign war with England. But in the meantime, we shall carry on an incessant and perpetual warfare with the Power of England in public and in secret.

The warning followed.

> You will note with pleasure that the informer is foredoomed, and that no man can betray and live.

Promises of continued secret warfare were fulfilled in October. Explosions occurred on the London underground railway. No lives were lost, but the considerable public alarm showed the Clan members that they were getting something for their money.

Patrick O'Donnell was hanged on 17 December 1883. The trial, and the inevitable verdict, suited the Fenian movement very well; martyrs were always welcome. In the following February, justifying himself in the course of a squabble over the money subscribed to the O'Donnell Defence Fund, Patrick Ford wrote in the *Irish World* of the trial:

> It made O'Donnell famous throughout the world—fit subject for the pen of fire of even Victor Hugo. It nerved the heart of the Avenger himself to ascend the scaffold with intrepid step, and, smiling at death, swing into eternity for Ireland. Finally, it has served notice on all would-be informers that the word of the British Empire, powerful though it be, is not potent enough to save them, and that the hand that executes vengeance upon them will be glorified for ages while they will be damned for ever in infamy.

Le Caron clipped the article and posted it, with other material, to Anderson.

19

Everywhere Betrayed

Le Caron practised medicine, managed three drug stores (two in Braidwood and one in Brace Hill, Illinois), and reported on the Fenian movement, yet he constantly sought to extend his scope. Here is how he exuberantly describes his activities in the 1880s.

> I made many trips to various points of the country, and so was enabled to gauge pretty accurately the condition of public feeling and the probabilities of the future. My pretexts for all this travelling were admirably adapted to divert suspicion from my real object. When a journey for my health's sake was not possible, I got appointed (through Irish political influence) to a seat on the Mississippi Valley Sanitary Commission; and when no more work was to be done under this cover, I connected myself with one of the largest pharmaceutical houses in the States, and travelled as their representative in whatever direction suited me. . . . When at home I was of course an ardent politician, and a volunteer on every committee in the Democratic interest. So prominent was I in local politics, that on one occasion I ran for election for the House of Representatives, only being defeated by a majority of 128 votes on a poll of several thousands. It was the cry of 'The Fenian General' that lost me the seat with the English voters.

He was at the Second Annual Convention of the Irish National League of America in 1884. The arrangements to control the meetings went as smoothly as before; however chaotic the Clan's workings in some respects, its planning and discipline were exemplary when running a front organization. On 13 August, before the proceedings opened, the caucus met in Codman Hall, Boston, the local camps' usual venue. Presiding, Dr Betts, the Episcopalian clergyman, raised a laugh by remarking that they would save the Convention delegates trouble by doing their work for them. While arranging for a majority of Clan-na-Gael members to be appointed to the National Committee of the League and the Executive Council, the caucus decided to change the president. Because Sullivan, by using the organization of the National League and the Clan for electioneering, had aroused hostility among some of the membership, it was agreed that on being renominated at the Convention he would announce his resignation and Patrick Egan be elected in his place. Egan's qualifications were excellent: a former treasurer of the Irish Land League, he had close connections with the Irish Parliamentary Party, he was active in the Clan, and he was in America as a fugitive from the British police hunt. With him in office, the Clan's position would be secure and Sullivan's actual influence undiminished.

A delegate from the Irish Party at Westminster, Mr Sexton, speaking of Sullivan, said to the public Convention: 'There is but one feeling concerning him in the hearts of the Irish race. He is a man who does honour to the race from which he sprung; he is a man of whom any race might well be proud.'

The change in presidency was no disadvantage to Le Caron. Egan admired and trusted him no less than did Sullivan, and he was later to give him a letter of introduction to 'all friends of the Irish National League': 'Dr Le Caron, although French by name and descent, has ever proved himself one of the most devoted Friends of the Irish National Cause, and since the formation of the Land and National Leagues has been most indefatigable in promoting the good of these organizations.'

At its secret caucus convention in September the Clan-na-Gael, while confirming the dynamite policy and approving measures for greater secrecy, reduced the executive body (the FC) to three (to be known to members as the Triangle) and gave itself the code name of US instead of VC. A circular issued by the new executive explained that no review of the past three years' operations would be made available as to do so would reveal the Clan's methods and imperil future operations. Nor were false claims to have carried out dynamite operations to be denied, as 'to deny in each case would be to affirm, which we cannot do and succeed in the work before us'. (O'Donovan Rossa—expelled from the Clan—and others were liable to claim responsibility each time a bomb was successfully exploded, and this presumption caused the Clan brothers to be what the circular called 'restive'.) Few, if any, circulars alluding to the work in progress were to be issued in future; members would learn of them from 'statements of the enemy through the press'.

Fearing that even these measures would not impress their loquacious followers, the leaders made yet another, and this time a rather desperate, appeal for caution:

> In conclusion, we instruct you peremptorily henceforth not to talk outside your halls of the business transacted there, or of anything concerning the organization. Men talk in the streets, on their way home, in saloons and elsewhere about our business. Some men think that loyalty to the organization compels them to talk about and defend it in presence of outsiders and of expelled members. This is wrong. The organization needs no defence. What it does need is silence. This *must* be secured.

The kind of brothers to whom these strictures were addressed can easily be imagined. They would not, however, unless personally involved, have learned any exact information about the most secret part of 'the work in course of progress'—the dynamite campaign. When, where and how bombs were to be placed had finally to be decided by the men on the spot. Devoy credited (or debited) Le Caron with responsibility for the arrest of twenty of the perpetrators. Anderson, however, denied that his agent had caused a single arrest, and claimed that he gave only general warnings. Le Caron had certainly supplied material on several of the dynamiters, including descriptions of Lomasney and Gallagher and the dates of their leaving America, but clearly he had not been able to give details of the times and sites of their operations, and nor had anybody else. Of the sporadic operations by the Rossa faction—including the spectacular blowing-up of a gasometer in Glasgow and explosions caused outside the *Times* office and the new building in Whitehall of the Local Government Board—Le Caron had no foreknowledge.

Later parties did better than Dr Gallagher, in that they reached their targets. In February 1884 an explosion occurred at Victoria Station. In May of that year a bomb considerably damaged the police offices in Scotland Yard. In December an attempt was made to blow up London Bridge but the explosive went off prematurely, killing William Mackey Lomasney and his brother Michael; in this case Sullivan had relaxed his rule of not sending men with families, and the Clan assumed responsibility for William's dependents. In January 1885 the Tower of London was attacked and a Clan agent, Luke Dillon, placed and detonated a bomb inside the House of Commons, which was not sitting at the time.

That the Fenian movement paid heavily in the loss of so many operatives was due to police work aided by informers. One of the men arrested in 1884 for being in possession of explosives, John Daly, suspected that he had been betrayed by 'Big Dan' O'Neill, a Liverpool Irishman. Several fellow prisoners would have echoed his lament, expressed in a letter from Winson Green Prison, Birmingham, to Devoy: 'It's damn hard, Jack, to think of the amount of traitors our business has produced, everywhere you turn, betrayed, betrayed.'

Le Caron's contribution was on a higher level, and the substance of the hundreds of reports he sent to London was incorporated in a secret 'Memorandum on the Organization of the United Brotherhood, or Clan-na-Gael in the United States', prepared for the Cabinet by Edward George Jenkinson, the Assistant Under-Secretary responsible for Secret Service work. Dated 22 January 1885, it covered in fourteen pages the history of the Clan-na-Gael, its organization and leading personalities, finances, relations with the National League, and dominant role in supporting the Irish Republican Brotherhood in Great Britain and Ireland. Jenkinson explained the Fenians' defence of their actions: 'Dynamite outrages and even assassinations are justified on the ground that the Irish race is at war with England, and are looked upon as acts of war. If life is lost no crime has been committed, as every war is unavoidably attended with loss of life.'

The memorandum is of particular interest as revealing that Whitehall had accepted the thesis constantly repeated by Le Caron and to be advanced in the near future by *The Times* in a famous series of articles. Jenkinson put it concisely for the Cabinet:

> Under the banner of the National League in America are ranged all the Irish Societies without distinction, so as to give to the world the idea that all Irishmen are united in the National cause, and that the League is the dominant Society. The National League in America

and in Great Britain and Ireland, the Parliamentary party under the leadership of Mr Parnell, the IRB, and the VC, are all working together with one common object in view, and the policy *publicly* set forth is to aid the Parliamentary party in its efforts to secure the independence of Ireland by constitutional means. But those who are working openly and on constitutional lines know perfectly well that they have secret organizations and a party of force at their backs. The mainspring of the whole movement is the VC.

Jenkinson's paper was written before the antagonisms inside the Clan became so acute that the outside world was made aware of them. Internal disputes inevitably arose from the organization's secret operations. Supporters who had contributed very large sums—$150,000 were collected within two years—wanted an account of the expenditure. The Triangle's case for secrecy was unanswerable, but the critics distrusted Sullivan and Egan, and they reproached the leadership with failing to pay the clandestine operators' expenses, to arrange for the defence of those captured, and to maintain widows and orphans. The dissidents' suspicions of where the money was going were strengthened when Sullivan had the account books burnt because they were, he alleged, in imminent danger of seizure by hostile forces.

Sullivan's most formidable opponent was Dr Patrick Henry Cronin, the bomb school instructor, a tall handsome man and a forceful speaker with a fine tenor voice. To stifle his accusations of embezzlement, Sullivan charged him in 1885 with treason before a disciplinary court—a senior member of which was Le Caron.

Ever since his admission to the VC Le Caron had been closely associated with Sullivan, and he knew that embezzlement was only one of his sponsor's crimes. His sole concern was to back the winner; Sullivan was the stronger man who would keep the majority with him. Accordingly he voted for Cronin's expulsion.

20

The Black Bag

In April 1886 Edward Caulfield Houston presented himself at Printing House Square, London, for an interview with the editor of *The Times*, George Earle Buckle, a well-proportioned man of 31, six feet tall (an exceptional height at that time), a barrister and a firm Protestant. It was a meeting between two ardent young campaigners. Houston, as secretary of the anti-Home Rule society, the Irish Loyal and Patriotic Union, was pursuing the inquiries he began after reporting the trial of the Phoenix Park murderers. Buckle's paper was opposing the Home Rule Bill then being introduced by Gladstone.

The 23-year-old Houston, bearing three testimonials to his integrity from men of repute, impressed the editor as highly intelligent and a strong character. Buckle felt dubious, however, about Houston's proposition that if the paper would advance the money he could procure letters revealing Parnell's opinions so starkly that they would gravely compromise the Irish leader. Too much mystery surrounded the proposed deal for Buckle's liking; who now owned the letters could not be disclosed for fear of his being murdered, and Houston knew of their contents only by hearsay. Cautiously Buckle told the caller that if he produced the originals purchase might be considered.

Houston had learned of the letters' existence from an elderly Irish journalist, Richard Pigott. Longer experience in Dublin journalism would have made him wary of Pigott. In the nature of his quest he could not invite opinions from possible rivals, so he did not discover that even among pressmen not remarkable for their high moral standards Pigott was considered rather disreputable. A less ardent researcher might have been put off by a story that the letters were in a black bag left behind in Paris by Frank Byrne, and procurable only by following a procedure directed by Pigott.

The young man enlisted the co-operation of a prominent Irish Unionist who, although older, was no more acquainted with Pigott's shady world than he was. Dr Maguire, Professor of Moral Philosophy at Trinity College, Dublin, accompanied Houston to a Paris hotel. After dark Pigott appeared furtively and, whispering through a large beard, said that two men, whom he named as Murphy and Brown, were waiting downstairs, and it was a condition of the transaction that they should not be seen. Houston and Maguire could examine the letters, and if satisfied they were to hand Pigott £500 in cash. Pigott would then take the money downstairs while they remained behind. Maguire, after inspecting the letters, agreed with Houston that they looked authentic. Pigott was given the money.

Houston was back in the *Times* office in late September with five letters purportedly signed by Parnell and five by Patrick Egan. Although convinced of their authenticity, he invited Buckle to subject them to any tests he pleased before paying the £1,780 he had expended in obtaining them. The editor consulted the manager, John Cameron MacDonald, the proprietor, John Walter, and the paper's solicitor, Joseph Soames. All agreed that the correspondence would make such an impact if published that the utmost care must be exercised before it was used.

One letter, written on a folded sheet of stout white paper, was so damning that it provided the complete case against Parnell. The paper itself, investigation showed, helped to confirm the letter's authenticity as it bore a long-discontinued watermark identifying it as having been supplied only to the Dublin Land League. The text was written in a clerkly hand on the first page, presumably by a secretary, as was usual in that pre-typewriter era. It was dated 15/5/82, no sender's address was given and the recipient was not named. It read:

> Dear Sir, I am not surprised at your friend's anger but he and you should know that to denounce the murders was the only course open to us. To do that promptly was plainly [here a repetition of the words *the only course* was deleted] our best policy.

But you can tell him and all others concerned that though I regret the accident of Lord F Cavendish's death I cannot refuse to admit that Burke got no more than his deserts.

You are at liberty to show him this, and others whom you can trust also, but let not my address be known. He can write to House of Commons.

The first page was filled by this writing, with no room at the bottom for a signature. Near the top right-hand corner of the back was written, in two lines, 'Yours very truly Chas. S Parnell'.

At Printing House Square the letter received the minutest attention. That it was signed on the fourth page was considered to be a precaution, so that the half-sheet might be torn off and the contents disclaimed. What had to be established beyond doubt was the genuineness of the signature.

Parnell was a reluctant letter-writer and examples of his signature were not readily obtainable. The Speaker refused to allow Soames to inspect the Test Roll signed by all newly elected members of the House of Commons, and ultimately *The Times* had to have recourse to its own Agony Column. A small advertisement appeared in the issue of 21 December 1886, headed AUTOGRAPHS WANTED, offering £10 for a collection of not less than twenty autographs of distinguished parliamentary leaders including those of Mr Gladstone, Lord Hartington, Sir William Harcourt, Mr Bright, Mr Chamberlain, Lord Salisbury, Lord Randolph Churchill, Mr Parnell, Mr Sexton and Sir M. Hicks-Beach. Collections were required within the next fortnight and were to be addressed to J.C.M., care of a well-known agency, Sampson Low and Company, in Fleet Street. This ruse produced three Parnell signatures within a week and others arrived later. Comparison of these seemed to confirm that the signature was Parnell's. Among the persons accepting its genuineness was the leading handwriting expert, George Smith Inglis, whom the Treasury consulted in prosecutions.

In January 1887 *The Times* paid Houston his price. On legal and other grounds it was decided not to publish the letter at once but to lead up to this devastating exposure by a series of articles.

Headlines in the modern sense had yet to be evolved. Newspaper readers were not told the substance of an article in a few captions;

they had to read it. The title of the series was 'Parnellism and Crime' and each section was introduced by a laconic headline: A RETRO-SPECT: IRELAND; A RETROSPECT: AMERICA; A STUDY IN CONTEMPORARY CONSPIRACY. Opening sentences were not designed to startle; writers approached their task in stages, allowing themselves plenty of space for reflections on the way. Thus *The Times* began its campaign on 7 March 1887 with a long leading article containing this splendid admonition.

> There is a great deal of flabby sentimentalism at the present day, which takes the form of flat refusal to believe that anybody can be very bad. It does not spring from any noble or even respectable root, for it is accompanied by equally conspicuous incapacity to think anybody very good. It is merely a product of sheer dullness of imagination and bluntness of perception. People are carefully shielded in this country from the machinations of the diabolically wicked, and the uneventful current of their daily lives does little to open up to them the possibilities of either good or evil in the human heart.

The word 'sensational' was just starting to be used, although rather cautiously, by the more popular papers. *The Times* did not apply this description to its attack on the Irish Parliamentary Party and the Home Rulers, but it would have been justified in doing so. A century later campaigning journalism can show nothing more vigorous and downright. The paper's judgement of Parnell and his allies could not have been more clearly expressed. 'In times not yet remote they would assuredly have been impeached for one tithe of their avowed defiance of the law, and in ages yet more robustly conscious of the difference between evil and good their heads would have decorated the City gates.'

John Woulfe Flanagan, the author of the first three articles, was the paper's chief leader-writer. The son of an Irish judge, he was a Catholic but a strong Unionist. At that time he was 35, and a formidable journalist. In carrying out this assignment he made telling use of extracts from Fenian papers, especially Patrick Ford's *Irish World*, and of public speeches both by acknowledged Fenians and Parnell's followers. His indictment was carefully planned; the opening articles contained significant pointers to what was to come later.

Any issue of the *Irish World* was liable to horrify, if not to scare, English readers. Ford exulted over 'the political agent called Dynamite' and he 'claimed the merit for Ireland' of first resorting to it; he referred to murders as executions and foresaw widespread devastation and arson in English cities; he gave much space to a contributor, Thomas Mooney, who wrote under the name of 'Trans-Atlantic', whose highly intemperate prose Flanagan described as 'homicidal ravings'. Having planted this impression of the *Irish World* in his readers' minds, Flanagan quoted a telegram sent by Parnell on 26 January 1881: 'Thanks to the *Irish World* and its readers for their constant co-operation and substantial support in our great cause.' At the same time Flanagan took a swipe at Gladstone for describing the huge sums sent from America to Ireland as 'only to carry on a public, legal, Parliamentary struggle.'

Flanagan then sowed doubts about the genuineness of Parnell's condemnation of the Phoenix Park murders. On Saturday 6 May 1882, Parnell, who had left Kilmainham Prison on 2 May, and Michael Davitt, released from Portland Prison earlier that day, were met at Vauxhall by 'Mr Frank Byrne and other favoured disciples'. That evening Cavendish and Burke were murdered with amputating knives brought (according to evidence at the trial) to Dublin for that purpose by Frank Byrne's wife. Parnell, Davitt and Dillon signed a manifesto recording their horror, but on the same day one of Parnell's followers, J. E. Redmond MP, in a speech at Manchester, condemned the murder of Cavendish but made no reference to Burke—'a point of high significance', remarked Flanagan. Its significance was to be heavily underlined later on.

Apart from the informer Carey's evidence in court (which had particularly stirred Houston to action), plenty of other shocking material existed, of which Flanagan made skilful use. In January 1882 Daniel Connell had sworn at Cork that 'he was offered a Parnell medal for bravery', and that his superior, 'Captain Moonlight', had got a medal. These decorations were awarded for actions set out in a 'regimental order': 'Thomas Sullivan to be shot in the legs; the mother and daughter's hair to be clipped for dealing with Hogarty, of Millstreet; and John Lehane, for story-telling to Father Twomey, to be clipped also. John Murphy to be shot in the legs for paying his rent.' P. J. Sheridan, one of Parnell's organizers, had taken part in forming the 'Patriotic Brotherhood', in whose books appeared, under the date 24 May 1882, the entry: 'At the request of the Land League, conveyed through Thomas Murphy, men have been sworn in specially to kill Mr Brooke.'

In what Flanagan termed 'the sympathetic atmosphere of New York' Parnell's supporters had lost their reticence. Matt Harris MP, described by Parnell as his 'tried and trusted' supporter, had observed that from an Irish standpoint 'the taking-off of Cavendish' was 'an execution, not a murder'. Patrick Egan, 'Mr Parnell's sagacious treasurer and colleague', had suggested a Martyrs' Fund 'as an incentive to other men to dare and do likewise for Ireland', and at a meeting to support the fund Frank Byrne

> . . . laid bare the pith and marrow of League doctrine in a few trenchant words. 'I am not', he said, 'fastidious as to the methods by which the cause of liberty may be advanced. (Applause.) I do not say you should alone use dynamite, or the knife, or the rifle, or Parliamentary agitation; but I hold no Irishman true who won't use all and each method as the opportunity presents itself.'

The third article was designed to show that the constitutional movement in the United Kingdom and the Fenian movement in the United States had always been, and still were, controlled by dynamiters and assassins, despite recent claims of Parnellites that the *Irish World* was now hostile to them. Packed with quotations and references as it was, it was not easy reading, but the attention of even superficial readers would have been caught by a report from the *Irish World* of what Flanagan called an 'inhuman feast . . . unsurpassed for cold-blooded ferocity in the annals of Christendom'. The occasion was a banquet on 6 May 1885, the anniversary of the Phoenix Park murders, in honour of Mrs Frank Byrne. Since Byrne and his wife had fled to the United States to avoid a charge of complicity, their innocence had been protested on numerous occasions, and members of Parnell's parliamentary party had in 1883 signed a testimonial to Byrne's character containing such sentences as: 'That we declare that down to the last Mr F. Byrne has continued to maintain a most legal and constitutional attitude in every respect, and we express our complete confidence in Mr Byrne's ability to refute every charge if he receives just and fair treatment.' Now, two years later, at 'one of the happiest Irish national reunions that has taken place in New York in some time', attended by a 'brilliant gathering of ladies and gentlemen', it was admitted that Mrs Byrne had had something—although exactly what was not specified—to do with the murder. The chairman, Austin Ford, described the guest of the evening as 'one who was an important, though most unpretending, actor in the event that is marked by the 6th of May' and as 'a brave little woman whose memorable courage in connexion with the victory in the Phoenix Park three years ago (prolonged applause) is known to us all'. Mrs Byrne's reward was what the reporter called 'a well-filled purse'. Modestly declining to make a speech herself, Mrs Byrne left that duty to her husband who (the summary is Flanagan's) 'returned thanks for the blood-money, exulted in the foul slaughter for which his wife was paid, and avowed that he relied on "modern improvements" of the rifle for his country's liberation'. During the oratory which followed, a speaker referred to one of the assassins, Joe Brady, as 'the modern Coriolanus, who struck a great blow for liberty'.

This article appeared on 14 March. A week had now passed since *The Times* launched its attack. The accusations were so assembled and worded that Parnell might have been expected to react furiously to even the first. He said nothing. Apart from a few public references by Irish Members of Parliament to 'old' and 'stale' charges (terms customarily used by politicians when they do not wish to go into details), no response came from the Irish leader and his party. If Parnell had acted as the leading men in Printing House Square thought he should, he would have sued for libel, when he could have been questioned in court and the defence would then have produced those letters so dramatically retrieved by Houston from the black bag in Paris.

Four days later the paper in a long leading article tried to prod Parliament into putting pressure on Parnell: 'We cannot believe that the House will allow any section of its members to treat with an affectation of indifference such statements as those deliberately advanced and supported by detailed evidence in the articles we have recently printed on "Parnellism and Crime".' The article urged Gladstone and his associates to make their position clear. It went on to issue a challenge: 'We have not yet learned that any one of the personages incriminated is about to institute legal proceedings against us, though if our charges could be shown to be unfounded and not for the public benefit, we presume MR PARNELL and his friends might ask for heavy damages.'

Nearly a month passed and still no one took the bait. On 12 April an article on the effects of the boycott appeared. It was a story of widespread intimidation, of murder, arson, maiming of people and cattle, of the isolation of families to the extent that no doctor, midwife or priest dared visit them, no one buy their produce or sell them the necessaries of life, no one bury their dead. Now a voice was raised in Parliament: Colonel Saunderson, a representative of the Protestants in Ulster, where, as *The Times* put it, 'social order continues to flourish undisturbed', accused the Nationalists not of having themselves 'imbrued their hands with blood' but of associating with men they knew to be murderers. This speech caused a 'scene', in which an Irish Member was suspended, and Saunderson had later to modify his statement. But no writ arrived in Printing House Square. Parnell's friends were advising him not to sue, either in London or Dublin, because a London jury would be certain to find against him and a favourable verdict by a Dublin jury would have no effect on English opinion.

On 18 April the hotly contested Coercion Bill, designed to give the Irish executive extended powers to deal with certain classes of crime, was due for its second reading. That morning *The Times* published the letter in facsimile 'by a process the accuracy of which cannot be impugned'. An accompanying article suggested that the 'Dear Sir' to whom the letter was addressed was Patrick Egan, and contrasted Parnell's speeches deploring the Phoenix Park murders with his real views as expressed in the letter. The letter was also dealt with in a leader which began: 'We place before our readers to-day a document the grave importance of which it would be difficult to over-estimate.' The subject of this exposure, which must have been the main topic of conversation that day in Westminster, Fleet Street, and over numerous breakfast tables, did not see the paper until the evening. Even then he seemed unperturbed, and it was his followers who induced him to repudiate the letter. Shortly after one o'clock in the morning, speaking from his place in the Chamber, he protested at 'a villainous and barefaced forgery'. It was a spirited speech, which at times had his supporters cheering and the House laughing appreciatively. 'I cannot understand how the conductors of a responsible, and what used to be a respectable journal could have been so hoodwinked, so hoaxed, so bamboozled, and that is the most charitable interpretation which I can place on it, as to publish such a production as that as my signature,' he declared.

Parnell made no threats of a court action, but he hit back further by repeating his accusations of forgery to news agencies' representatives. A long argument ensued in *The Times* about the characteristics of Parnell's signature, the lack of a stop after the middle initial, and the substance of the letter, during which the paper insisted that the document was genuine and that its sentiments were consistent with the unanswerable case it had made against Parnell.

While these charges and counter-charges were being published, Le Caron arrived in London.

21

Agent versus Agent

A lull occurred in the dynamite campaign after the explosions at the Tower of London and the House of Commons in January 1885. Le Caron explains it as a diplomatic pause consequent on the introduction of Gladstone's Home Rule Bill. He was not a delegate to a secret convention of the Sullivan faction in August 1886, but reports he received revealed that the executive, while staying its hand, was collecting funds and preparing to resume its activities. Relative quiet still prevailed when in April 1887 Le Caron, this time without introductions or credentials, visited London.

He did not see Parnell again but he called on Irish Members of Parliament. One member, Dr James G. Fox, passed him in the lobby without recognizing him, although they had met at conventions in America. Fox had lived in Troy for fifteen years and served as State Executive for the Land League in New York. Le Caron decided to investigate whether Fox belonged to the Clan-na-Gael.

Ascertaining that his quarry frequently dined at Gatti's Restaurant in the Strand, he seated himself at the same table. Fortunately Fox was reading the *Irish World*, so Le Caron found it easy to open a conversation by asking, in his strongest American accent, whether he could obtain copies in London. Fox knew of no local source, as he received the paper direct, but they introduced themselves and agreed that they must have met at conventions. Le Caron gave him the Clan 'hailing sign' to which there was no response, although Fox remarked 'significantly' (as Le Caron thought) that he was not a member of any secret society. They parted without Le Caron having found out what he wanted to know.

Anderson took advantage of Le Caron's presence to send him to Paris to see a prominent Clan-na-Gael member, General F. F. Millen. This was a case of a British agent being sent to check on another British agent, both of whom were high in the Fenian counsels.

Millen was born in County Fermanagh. He served in the Liberal Army of the Republic of Mexico and gained experience as a senior officer. In the Fenian movement in America he claimed, and was accorded, the rank of General. In 1865 he was entrusted with the task of equipping an Irish army in Ireland, in the following year he was a member of the Clan-na-Gael delegation to the Russian ambassador in Washington to seek military aid, and in 1879, travelling under the alias of General Morgan, he accompanied John Devoy on a secret mission to Irish Republican Brotherhood centres in Ireland to inspect their military organization.

While he was highly regarded by the Fenians as a military expert, he formed a low opinion of the Republican movement's leaders. Early encounters with the men claiming to be the liberators and future rulers of Ireland shocked him. He had expected to meet educated gentlemen, who would not have seemed out of place in Parliament or in Pall Mall clubs, who could have represented Ireland on equal terms with the emissaries of other governments. In 1865 he called on E. M. Archibald, the British Consul in New York; it was, apparently, a tentative approach, and he was not explicit about his purpose. In 1866 he called again, and Archibald was sufficiently impressed to write to London, using for Millen the alias of Francis Martin. Shortly afterwards Millen handed Archibald a breakdown of the Fenian centres in Ireland and the names of men in the United States who had volunteered to go to Ireland to take part in an armed uprising. From time to time he received money—sometimes as much as £250—from British secret funds.

Like Le Caron, he was entrusted by Alexander Sullivan with important assignments. In 1887 Sullivan sent him to Paris. London, keeping a wary eye on the General, wanted to know what this trip was about, and the arrival of Le Caron, a wholly trustworthy agent, was opportune. If Le Caron knew of Millen's dealings with the British, he gives no hint of it in his book; such a revelation would have been deleted anyway during the vetting of the manuscript. Certainly Millen knew nothing of his visitor's undercover role.

Millen was staying in the Hôtel des Anglais in the Cour de la Reine with his wife and two daughters. Le Caron's excuse for this visit was that he had heard of the General's presence in Paris through the *Herald* office and was anxious as an old friend to greet him. London had suspected that Millen's trip was connected with future dynamite attacks but Le Caron ascertained that, at least on this occasion, Millen was not in touch with dynamiters. Sullivan's aim was to improve relations between his faction and the Irish Republican Brotherhood. The Irish disapproved of the American-directed bombing campaign in England because they feared that it would cause the Government to impose more repressive measures in Ireland and that there would be a backlash against the Irish living on the British mainland. Accordingly Sullivan had cut off their funds and ceased to invite their representatives to conventions in the United States. Now, in view of the dissensions among the American-Irish, Sullivan aimed to get ahead of his rivals by patching up his differences with the home movement. The representatives from Ireland, however, wanted an assurance, which Millen was unable to give, that the bombing campaign would not be resumed, so relations remained distant. On his return Millen presented an optimistic report which his negotiations had not justified.

Even while these discussions were proceeding in Paris, funds were being raised in America for what was called a firework display to enliven the celebration of Queen Victoria's Jubilee that summer. For this occasion the Sullivan and Rossa factions had joined forces, the former to supply the funds and the latter the operatives. An explosion was to occur during the thanksgiving service at Westminster Abbey and a second attack to be made on the Houses of Parliament. Millen was charged with the overall supervision, and he returned to Paris, while a small team landed in England. Le Caron was not asked to go back to Paris, nor was his presence there necessary. Scotland Yard's Special Branch shadowed the dynamiters from the time they disembarked. When one of them had his moustache and beard shaved off at a barber's, a detective was waiting outside to note his changed appearance. Even a brief stay in a café to drink a cup of coffee was meticulously logged. Two of them, Thomas Callan, a labourer, and a grocer, Michael Harkins, stayed in separate lodgings at about six shillings a week each—accommodation not to be compared with Millen's comfortable base at the Hôtel des Anglais. The team was reduced by the death, from illness, of one man. No explosions took place and the celebrations were unmarred. The leader of the party, one of Sullivan's friends named John J. Monroney, who used the alias Joseph Melville, escaped, but Callan and Harkins were sentenced to fifteen years' imprisonment.

Millen did not set foot in England. According to a newspaper story, a British detective at Boulogne warned him that he would be arrested if he did. Two interpretations of this incident are possible. Special Branch might have given Millen this friendly tip as a reward for his services, at the same time saving themselves the embarrassment of having an informer questioned in court. Or the encounter with the detective might have been stage-managed and leaked to the press to provide Millen with cover for his return to his possibly suspicious Fenian sponsors after a failed mission. Someone on the inside of the plot had certainly given the police all the information they needed; Chief Inspector Adolphus Frederick Williamson, in his statement for the prosecution, said, 'I am in possession of information'; and, later, Chief Inspector John Mallon, the senior Dublin detective, said that 'Millen humbugged them'.

His investigation of Fox and his visit to Millen were minor jobs for Le Caron. The important event of that year was his contribution by proxy to the press attack on Parnell. On 13 May 1887, *The Times* began the publication of three articles—anonymous, as was the practice with all contributions—under the heading BEHIND THE SCENES IN AMERICA, which consisted of Le Caron's material written up by Robert Anderson. Civil servants, under a Treasury Rule of 1875, republished in 1884, were forbidden to write for the press without permission, so Anderson should have had the consent of his superior, James Monro, the Assistant Commissioner of the Metropolitan Police. Anderson maintained later that he had permission, but Monro denied it. The discrepancy probably illustrates the informal atmosphere of secret work. Monro wisely left Anderson a free hand to run his agent and Anderson—understandably in the kind of operation he was engaged in—was contemptuous of bureaucratic restrictions. The two men were on friendly terms and dined at each other's houses; it is possible that Anderson casually mentioned his journalistic project while they faced each other from armchairs and that Monro nodded. But, as every civil servant knows, no agreement is valid without a signature, and the arrangement, if it existed, was never put into writing.

Civil service protocol was none of Buckle's business; to him the articles were a powerful reinforcement of his case. Although they lacked the eloquence, the fire and the scorn of Flanagan's prose, the evidence they provided was irrefutable. Anderson's problem was to present the information without compromising the source. He seized on the disputes then proceeding within the Clan-na-Gael to explain the paper's possession of 'the secret records of the American conspirators'.

> The following is the result of an inquiry instituted last summer into this special subject. The time has proved exceptionally opportune for such an investigation. The great Clan-na-Gael Society, which till lately has maintained with extraordinary success the secrecy of its plots and methods, has shared at last the fate of all Irish associations of the kind. A feud within its ranks has led to a secession of many of its foremost men, some of whom were among the most influential of its founders. The schism has been embittered, moreover, by the element of personal quarrels between rival leaders. It has been possible, therefore, to secure a number of important documents, including copies of the 'Constitution' of the society and printed lists of the officers at various epochs, letters from past and present leaders, secret reports of conventions, and secret circulars issued from time to time by the executive and preserved in violation of definite rules and solemn pledges. The inquiry is still incomplete, for the society has lately been re-organized under a new secret name, and upon such a basis as to ensure greater secrecy than ever, and its present proceedings are veiled in seemingly impenetrable mystery. But the results already obtained are so important and so startling, and, moreover, they throw so much light upon recent events and present agitation at home, that it seems desirable, without further delay, to place them before the public.

As Le Caron was not a dissident, but an apparently loyal supporter of the Sullivan-Egan faction and a member of the even more secret reorganized society, he was unlikely to come under suspicion, whereas it must have seemed highly probable that one of Sullivan's numerous enemies had passed the documents to a hostile investigator. No hint was given in the articles that much of the material had been in London for years.

Tracing the history of the Clan-na-Gael, the writer permitted himself a reference to 'the contemptible failure of the Fenian raid on Canada in 1870'. From there, supporting every assertion with quotations, he went on to reveal the internal affairs of the Clan, the change of front which resulted in the New Departure, and the tactical moves by which the National League of America was taken over. Readers of *The Times* were told more than had ever been disclosed by the executive to the rank and file members of the Clan.

Three months after the opening article, on 7 June, *The Times* was still trying to provoke Parnell.

> All the information now laid before the public in a compact form, upon the unimpeachable authority of the conspirators themselves, goes to enforce the lesson of the New Departure and the previous revelations of the connexion between Parnellism and crime. The whole conspiracy, whether carried on by mealy-mouthed gentlemen who sit at London dinner-tables, or by the fiends who organize arson and murder, is one and indivisible.

22

The Witness Makes his Will

'Here was pandemonium let loose for eight days, during which the Convention sat morning, noon and night. I was a member of this assembly and I never heard such a row in my life.'

Le Caron is describing the secret assembly in June 1888 when the two sections of the United Brotherhood met in Chicago to attempt a reunion. Since 1886 the movement's fortunes had been drooping and many camps (including Le Caron's at Braidwood) were barely justifying their existence. The meeting of the Joint Committee on Credentials began with a dispute over the admission of delegates. Dr Cronin asserted that Triangle delegates were present from clubs which were no longer in being. As delegates' applications were reviewed, he sharply attacked Le Caron, alleging that the Braidwood club had ceased to meet and that native American doctors regarded him unfavourably. During the argument, which went on nearly all night, Le Caron sat next to Egan and was seen to be exchanging whispered comments with him. When John Devoy opposed a proposition on the grounds that it would give an advantage to British spies, Egan looked straight at him and hissed: 'We know where the British spies are!' Le Caron was eventually admitted on the recommendation of the local district officer.

The meeting place had already been changed because of suspected penetration by British detectives but the subject of espionage flared up again when a delegate, described by Le Caron as 'burly', stood up waving a pamphlet entitled 'Behind the Scenes in America'. It was a reprint, priced one penny, of the articles based on Le Caron's material, and issued in this form to state the paper's case beyond its own readership. (The complete 'Parnellism and Crime' series was republished in stiff covers for a shilling.) Mounting a chair a few feet away from Le Caron the man, announcing that he was from Troy, told the meeting that this little book had been sent to him by a member of the British Parliament who belonged to his camp. The information it contained could have been supplied only by a traitor high in the organization, and he moved the appointment of a committee of inquiry.

Unruffled, Le Caron was recalling to himself the conversation across the table at Gatti's Restaurant. Fox had lived in Troy. What Le Caron had failed to establish in London had, it seemed, been revealed here.

The Troy delegate's proposal of a committee was adopted but its inquiry was unavailing. By accepting that the information could have been supplied only by a highly placed member, the Troy delegate had endorsed the pamphlet's authenticity.

Devoy repeated his suspicions about hostile agents during the Convention, alleging that a spy at the 1881 Convention had reported the proceedings to the British Consul in New York. This man, Devoy added, was an officer in the organization and was probably listening to him in the present meeting. Devoy was doubtless correct in both assertions, but he did not have Le Caron in mind, as he admitted when recounting an incident as the delegates made their way out. He fell in with Le Caron and 'gave him a little tongue thrashing, asking him what the English had done to him, a Frenchman—which we all then supposed him to be—that he was so very anxious to blow them all up. He was exceedingly nervous and hurried away from me as quickly as he could. He evidently thought I suspected his real character or had information which I had not.'

Le Caron was in Sullivan's office, in the Opera House building, when Joseph O'Byrne, acting for the anti-Triangle group represented by Luke Dillon and John Devoy, walked in to deliver, as laid down in the organization's rules, copies of the charges against the Triangle—Sullivan, Michael Boland and Denis C. Feely. O'Byrne reported to his associates on his return that Sullivan and Le Caron had been conferring together, confirming their view that he was an intimate member of the Sullivan team.

A trial committee was set up (surprisingly Cronin, who was one of those making the charges, was a member of it). Le Caron describes his own part:

> I figured in this trial by furnishing Sullivan with affidavits for his defence. Cronin afterwards charged Sullivan with getting me admitted into the organization, and with putting me into a position of trust. This did not help matters, and altogether Cronin proved himself to be a very dangerous man in the eyes of Sullivan.

The committee could not reach a unanimous conclusion: four were for an acquittal and two (of whom Cronin was one) voted for a conviction. Cronin wanted the evidence published but the majority decided to withhold it.

At this time Le Caron was closely following events across the Atlantic. Someone had reacted to the 'Parnellism and Crime' articles, but from the paper's point of view it was the wrong man. He was Frank Hugh O'Donnell, a former Irish Member of Parliament then living in Germany. Writing to *The Times*, he denied any association of Parnell and his fellow members with the crimes of Byrne, the fugitive secretary of the Home Rule Confederation and Land League. The paper published a reply which O'Donnell, reading it in conjunction with 'Parnellism and Crime', interpreted as accusing him of complicity in Byrne's actions, and he sued *The Times* for libel. The hearing lasted from 2 to 5 July 1888 before Lord Coleridge, the Lord Chief Justice, and a special jury. The defence was that the plaintiff was not accused by name, that he was not one of the Irish leaders, and that he was attempting to raise a false issue and thus get the question of the letters tried without making Parnell or any of the real leaders a party to the case. Lord Coleridge refused to allow the general libels on the Irish party to be tried there and ruled that the issues be limited to the words relating to O'Donnell personally. It left O'Donnell with no case and the jury found for the defendants without leaving the box.

Although the case was dismissed, it had important repercussions, because during the hearing other letters purportedly written by Parnell were produced, and one of them, to Patrick Egan, pre-dating the Phoenix Park murders, appeared to be an incitement to violence. It began: 'What are these fellows waiting for? This inaction is inexcusable; our best men are in prison and nothing is being done.'

A collective request from the Irish Members for a government inquiry had been met by an official reply that the proper course was a suit for libel. After the O'Donnell case ended, Parnell acted at last, and events now began to move quickly. The Irish leader asked the House of Commons to appoint a Select Committee to inquire into the genuineness of the facsimile letter. The Government declined but offered to set up a Special Commission to examine all the charges in 'Parnellism and Crime'. The Bill to give effect to the proposal was opposed by the Home Rule Liberals and the Irish, who wished to limit the inquiry to the question of the letter. The Government used its majority to force the Bill's passage; it received the Royal Assent in August but before its passage into law prevented the prosecution of ordinary legal proceedings, Parnell started a libel action claiming £100,000 damages in the Court of Session in Edinburgh.

When Le Caron learned that the Government was setting up the Commission he wrote to Anderson offering to give evidence. Anderson was horrified at the idea that his agent should abandon his cover, destroy his usefulness, and risk being assassinated. For over twenty years Anderson had concealed his agent's existence, even from Scotland Yard, and—except for a few papers which could safely be passed into Home Office files—he had observed the agreement that the hundreds of documents sent from America should remain Le Caron's property, to be returned to him on demand. Now, if Le Caron appeared in public before the Commission, the whole story, which should never have been revealed at least during the agent's lifetime, would be in newspapers throughout the English-speaking world. While his concern for Le Caron's safety and continued usefulness was uppermost in his mind, Anderson was also doubtless bothered about his own position. As a civil servant, spending public money, he had behaved in a highly unorthodox manner. In civil service minds procedures are more important than results, however valuable. He rejected Le Caron's suggestion as unthinkable.

The Commissioners held a preliminary meeting on 17 September 1888. They were Sir James Hannen, President of the Probate, Divorce and Admiralty Court, Mr Justice Day and Mr Justice A. L. Smith. Justice Day was a Roman Catholic; because Nationalists suspected, or knew, that he was not a Home Ruler (English Catholics in general were not) he did not speak during the hearings. As revealed at this meeting, the Commissioners' concept of their duties caused dismay in Printing House Square, where the management had reckoned on a simple libel action, in which the issue would have been limited to the passages to which the plaintiff took exception and costs would have been recoverable by the successful party. What lay before the paper's management now was vastly different. The Commissioners decided that counsel for *The Times* must assume the prosecution's role and proceed as though the Irish Members were charged on an indictment containing all the matters alleged in 'Parnellism and Crime'. Thus the paper was to bear the burden of proof for every statement of fact contained in the articles, and quotations from Irish Nationalist journals would not be sufficient evidence; witnesses would have to appear in court for oral examination. The cost of conducting the prosecution and paying the expenses of hundreds of witnesses would fall upon *The Times*, without any possibility of recovering this enormous outlay even if the Commission found the charges proved.

Controversy surrounded the Commission. Allegations were made that Lord Salisbury's Government helped the prosecution in gathering evidence. John Daly, while serving a sentence in Chatham Prison, claimed to have been visited by Pigott and by Soames, the *Times* solicitor. Thomas J. Clarke, a fellow prisoner, related that he had been visited by Inspector Littlechild of Scotland Yard, who seemed to be offering him release and a job in the civil service if he would give evidence to the Parnell Commission. William Henry Joyce, transferred from the Royal Irish Constabulary in 1888 and appointed against his wish as a Resident Magistrate to conduct secret inquiries into an agitation against rent rises, asserted that he was switched from this task to collecting evidence supporting the charges. A man with a grievance, Joyce was anxious to give evidence for the defence at the Parnell Commission, but he was not called.

Le Caron wrote again to Anderson in September, urging the necessity of presenting a powerful case. Anderson was adamant; he repeated that Le Caron's appearance at a public inquiry was out of the question.

The Special Commission reopened its proceedings on 22 October 1888 in Number One Probate Court at the Royal Courts of Justice in the Strand. Sir Richard Webster, the Attorney-General, led for *The Times*; he was appearing as counsel for the paper and not in his official capacity, but he could avail himself of the resources of his office. He was assisted by three members of the English bar and two of the Irish bar. Sir Charles Russell MP and Herbert Asquith MP (later to be Prime Minister) represented Parnell. Other counsel appeared for members of the Irish Party. Michael Davitt conducted his own case.

Newspapermen and their readers had anticipated that the inquiry would open with an attack on Parnell and the production of damning documentary evidence. Instead, a lot of time was spent on the Land League, with quotations from numerous speeches and the interrogation of one dull witness after another. Reporters, trying to maintain readers' interest, occasionally mentioned that 'the letters' were still in the offing. In Braidwood, reading the newspaper reports, Le Caron feared that the Attorney-General's presentation was inadequate. Again he wrote to Anderson, emphasizing that he would accept all risks in appearing as a witness. It was now November, and despite its leisurely pace the Commission could not last for ever. Anderson still tried to dissuade him; if Le Caron came to London for this purpose it would, he wrote, be on his own responsibility.

Public interest in the Commission revived somewhat in December when Captain Boycott, already a legend, appeared as a witness and, speaking through a flowing moustache and wagging a large white beard, told of his isolation and the threats which had driven him from Mayo.

Le Caron was on his way to England; it was a journey he would have made at that time anyway, as his father was dying. Apart from his family and a few acquaintances, nobody would have remarked his arrival in Colchester; he was just the successful son of a former rate collector resident for years in Mersea Road. He had paused in London to see Anderson, who corrected an impression he had that the Government was prosecuting Parnell. Anderson explained the position of *The Times*, and pleaded with the visitor to change his mind. Le Caron reappeared the next week, declaring that he could not forget that he was an Englishman, that he had gone into the conspiracy to serve his country and now intended to see the matter through whatever the consequences. He wanted to be put in touch with *The Times*. Anderson said that he had had no communication with the paper concerning the Commission and would volunteer no assistance in the case. If he were applied to for help he would bear Le Caron's request in mind.

The appeal for help came in January from MacDonald, the manager of *The Times*. He wanted to find a witness to prove 'the American part of the case'; it was natural for him to suppose that the author of the series 'Behind the Scenes in America' had a good source, and he was approaching Anderson not as the head of the CID but as a knowledgeable contributor. Anderson was evasive but Le Caron, after his father's funeral, was pressing. Ultimately Anderson agreed to put his valuable witness in touch with some trustworthy person to be nominated by MacDonald, and the nominee was Houston.

In accordance with his original stipulation, Le Caron received his property back. Bearing a heavy packet of documents and a brief note written by Anderson introducing Mr Beach, and initialled 'R.A.', he took a cab to Houston's house at 3, Cork Street. There, for ten days, in a room dense with cigar smoke, the two men went through the pile of papers. When they broke up for the night, Houston stuffed them into his safe. In the end Le Caron, with Houston's agreement, selected about forty. On one sheet he observed that Anderson had written: 'Copy sent to Irish Office.—R.A.', and he snipped this note off so as not to bring Anderson into any discussion there might be. From one of his letters he deleted a page because it contained names he thought should be kept secret.

Houston informed the prosecution that a new witness was available, and Le Caron waited to be called. He cabled to his wife to come to England with his family and his papers. His son Henry and his eldest daughter, who was married, elected to remain in the United States. Nannie, accustomed through most of her married life to adapting herself to the exigencies of her husband's secret work, packed and booked—at the expense of *The Times*—passages to Liverpool for herself and four children.

Le Caron visited a Colchester solicitor, Asher Prior, to give instructions for his will to be drawn up.

23

Fame and Danger

'On Tuesday morning, the 5th of February 1889, the curtain was rung up, and throwing aside the mask for ever, I stepped into the witness-box and came out in my true colours, as an Englishman, proud of his country, and in no sense ashamed of his record in her service.'

Le Caron had chosen an impressive stage for his appearance. It was the forty-fourth day of the Special Commission, and word had gone round that what the newspapers now called 'the letters' were to be produced. The public seats—admission was by ticket—were more occupied than they had recently been. The press table was full. Precisely at half-past ten the judges entered. Some discussion about documents occurred, and then the Attorney-General announced that he was to take 'the American part' of the case. As he rose to call his new witness, some members of the public stirred, as though about to leave. Parnell was not in his place, and it was evident that the appearance of the letters had again been postponed. After hearing a few words, and seeing the man in the witness box, those who had thought of leaving decided to stay.

Mostly the journalists scarcely bothered to describe the witnesses, but they devoted their attention to this one. The *Daily News* representative wrote:

> Major Le Caron is short and slightish in build; neat, erect—like a soldier—cool as any cucumber; he has a well-shaped head, lofty forehead, and smallish, alert eyes, which look one level in the face.

With his arms folded over his chest—Napoleonically—he raps out his answers, short, sharp. 'Yes, yes,' he says, snappishly sometimes, pronouncing it 'yus'.

The *Morning Post* portrayed him as 'a sparsely-built man of medium height, with a sallow, determined face, clean shaven with the exception of a carefully-waxed dark moustache. He answered questions only after careful thought, generally standing with folded arms and erect bearing, and spoke rapidly, with only a slight American accent.' Commenting that 'Things were much livelier in the Commission Court yesterday,' the *Daily Chronicle* saw him as 'a little ferret-eyed, sharp-visaged person'. To the descriptive writer from the *Graphic* he spoke with 'a sharp metallic twang' and gave his evidence 'with great precision as well as frankness'.

Although he carefully articulated his baptismal names, reporters rendered Billis as Willis or Miller (Miller appears in the *Dictionary of National Biography*) and one called him Thomas Philip Leach. They differed, also, about a badge on the lapel of his black frock coat; it showed, in fact, his membership of the civil war veterans' organization, the Grand Army of the Republic. (He wore the medal for his portrait taken in Braidwood.)

Le Caron caused astonishment by the precision of his statements and his memory for names, dates and figures, as the Attorney-General took him through his career, starting with his joining the Northern Army, his meeting O'Neill, and the Fenian attack on Canada. When the Attorney-General asked: 'You communicated every detail to the Canadian Government?' he replied with such self-satisfaction that there was a general laugh. The witness revealed that he was still Senior Guardian of the Braidwood Camp, now re-numbered 121. (The two keys were in his pocket while he was giving evidence, and he had shown them to Houston.) He told the court the names of the Clan-na-Gael personalities, explained its cyphers, and described the escort of Clan armed guards attending Parnell and Dillon in Chicago in 1880; the tour, he insisted, was wholly under the Clan's direction. From the episode of the sealed packets which he carried to Paris, the Attorney-General guided him to the interview with Parnell in the House of Commons. Sir Charles Russell, who had already made various routine objections, looked up with an incredulous smile (unnoticed by Le Caron) at the statement

Le Caron in the witness box at the Parnell Commission identifying Parnell's portrait, as sketched by Sydney Prior Hall

attributed to Parnell: 'Doctor, I have long since ceased to believe that anything but the force of arms will ever bring about the redemption of Ireland.' The signed photograph given him by Parnell was, Le Caron said, now on the Atlantic and would probably be there tomorrow. By the time the Commission rose at four o'clock, Le Caron was describing his visit to Kilmainham Prison.

Press coverage the next day filled column after column of small type, and sub-editors even permitted themselves such—for the time—exciting headlines as 'Startling Evidence from America' and 'Extraordinary Revelations of a Spy'. Readers, who must have been skipping the tedious reports of the Commission were, in effect, told to look out for the next thrilling instalment. The *Daily Chronicle* summed up:

> The evidence of the witness is to be resumed to-day, and how important it is may be seen from the rapt attention which the Parnellite counsel pay to every syllable of it, as Major or Dr Le Caron clearly enunciates the words, with a very marked American accent, and with even more pronounced mannerisms. In spite of the danger he must feel that he runs from the revenge of at least the American section, he is as cool and collected in his answers as any man who ever took an oath, and his self-command and steadfast refusal to go one inch further than he can recollect is as remarkable as, it must be admitted, are his statements.

A Reuter telegram reported that Archbishop Ryan, of Philadelphia, had promised $100 to the Parnell Defence Fund.

The same issues contained the news that Parnell's action in the Edinburgh Court of Session had been dismissed on the ground that there was no jurisdiction, but that Parnell had given notice of an appeal.

Interest in America was no less. Dr William B. Carroll, mentioned by Le Caron in connection with the Skirmishing Fund, rushed to cable a denial to Parnell, and on the same day, 6 February, he wrote to Devoy:

> Who is this latest ruffian, 'Major Le Carron' or 'Dr Beach', who has turned up in the Parnell trial? Some scoundrel, I suppose, who has got into camps here, picked up the names he supposed were on the Directory, and got possession of some papers and reports and is

earning his money by making up a 'cock and bull' story for the *Times*.

I cabled Parnell this morning as follows: 'Le Carron's testimony concerning me absolutely false. Never heard of him before.' Of course, a mere cablegram, or for that matter an affidavit from one of us can have no influence on the Commission, but it will help the general, and particularly the Irish public, to understand the nature of the 'evidence' given.

On the following days the public seats were crowded with an attentive audience. Suddenly the Commission had become the biggest attraction in London, bringing into the court Oscar Wilde, Herbert Beerbohm Tree, Sir Frederick Leighton (President of the Royal Academy), Henry Labouchere MP (the founder and editor of *Truth*), Viscount Castlerosse, Mrs Gladstone, Lady Russell, Mrs Asquith, Mr Bridge (the Bow Street magistrate), numerous Members of Parliament, and so many society ladies that reporters commented on the fashionable assembly. Parnell, looking worn and haggard, usually came in very late, and sat at the solicitors' table. Houston attended the whole time, eagerly watching the culmination of his long quest.

The President, on the second day, noticed the pile of papers before the Attorney-General, guessed that the witness would be in the box all day, and said that he could give his evidence sitting down. Le Caron, although expressing his thanks, chose to stand while being questioned and to sit down during the frequent and lengthy reading of documents. As he was to do every day, Le Caron first corrected minor errors in the official report. The rest of the morning was taken up with a legal argument about the admissibility of evidence, during which the witness had to leave the box and the judges retired for half an hour.

The witness had plenty of opportunities to sit down, because counsel on both sides often insisted that documents and circulars should be read in full. At one point, after several circulars had been read and Sir Henry James was seen to be picking up yet another, the President remarked: 'It seems to me, and I think I have the concurrence of my learned brothers, that you have done enough with regard to these circulars.' 'I fear not, my lord,' Sir Henry replied. An argument ensued between the Attorney-General and Sir Charles

Russell, after which the President commented: 'It is very discouraging to me to find, when I desire to shorten the case, that I rather prolong it.'

Le Caron smiled broadly, and the audience laughed, when the Attorney-General read Egan's letter commending Le Caron as 'one of the strongest friends of the National cause, and indefatigable in promoting the organization', and there was another laugh when he explained that he was on the trial committee which expelled Dr Cronin for 'treason to Ireland and violation of his oath and obligations'. As his examination-in-chief was coming to a close, Le Caron wrote a note for the Attorney-General: 'You have not put in the paper called F.C. of 1888.' Sir Charles Russell demanded to see it and the Attorney-General handed it over with a sarcastic 'Certainly.' Sir Charles, looking at Le Caron, said: 'We are rather particular here.' Apologetically Le Caron remarked: 'I do not know the rules of the court. Perhaps I have done wrong,' upon which the President observed: 'We have no rules. Concerning yourself, you have only to answer questions.'

This was not the sole time that Le Caron was told merely to answer questions; thus he was prevented from giving information which the Commission was apparently seeking. To deny a witness the opportunity to volunteer statements implies that the questioner knows what questions to ask, and it became abundantly plain that both counsel and judges were confused—and understandably so—by the fearsome tangle of Irish revolutionary organizations and their internecine disputes, unable to sort out clearly the numerous individuals involved, and fatigued—James was once observed to have fallen asleep—by the reading aloud of so much Irish rhetoric. Questions were asked which led nowhere and objections raised which diverted the witness from his narrative.

Sir Charles Russell put on an impressive act when his turn came to examine Le Caron. To quote the *Morning Post:* 'Never since the Commission opened has the Court presented a more striking spectacle than when Sir Charles Russell rose to commence his cross-examination. Every seat was occupied, the gangways were crowded, and there was an expectant silence. Sir Charles put up his seat, leaned against the desks behind him, and opened the ball in conciliatory tones.' Only twenty minutes remained of the afternoon before the proceedings closed. Sir Charles, addressing the witness as Mr

Beach, seemed concerned to establish that he was of lowly origin, a rate collector's son who had started life as a draper's assistant. In the final question that day he suddenly returned to this subject, asking whether he had had any other employer than William Baber and receiving the answer that he had been apprenticed at 13 to James Knight. In the meantime Sir Charles had put several questions about why the witness took the Fenian oath and stopped him when he wished to add an explanation. After Sir Charles asked with whom he had arranged 'to betray the information you obtained', he interrupted twice as soon as the witness started a sentence. On the third interruption the Attorney-General protested: 'Let him answer.' Sir Charles then asked six more questions, with slightly altered wording, to all of which Le Caron replied that the communication was with his father. Later, under further questioning about the oath and his position in the Fenian movement, he managed to interject: 'I looked upon myself as a military spy in the service of my country.' After several questions about where the documents had recently been, and the intervention of the President, Le Caron was forced, very reluctantly, to mention Anderson's name, and to agree that he had been to Houston's home.

The Irish party were in high spirits when the hearing closed. They felt that battle had been joined at last. Crowding round Parnell and Russell, they became, as one journalist put it, 'downright merry'.

Both parties addressed each other with studied politeness when the cross-examination resumed the next morning. Sir Charles returned, for no clear reason, to the subject of the transfer of the letters from Anderson to Beach (as he continued to call him) and then to Houston. 'Why there should have been any mystery about this very natural proceeding, seeing the witness had volunteered his evidence to *The Times*, is not apparent, and the question of interest to the public would seem to be not how the evidence was obtained, but is the evidence true,' the *Daily Chronicle* observed. Russell wanted to see Anderson's note of introduction, but Houston had not kept it. Le Caron said he did not think it was signed. At this point Le Caron, maintaining that he had come to England on his own initiative, remarked that on reading reports of the Commission, 'I saw what I considered a lame presentation of the prosecution.' Loud laughter greeted this comment, the Attorney-General joining in, and it was renewed when Russell observed: 'That is very hard on the Attorney-General.'

Russell's tactic was to alternate courtesy with innuendo and bullying. When Le Caron, referring to Anderson's introductory note, said: 'It has just occurred to my mind that it was initialled "R.A.", Russell interjected: 'Oh, just occurred to your mind.' On Le Caron's correction of a date, given from memory, by one year, Russell implied that this was an example of prevarication. Russell took up a good deal of time complaining that slip one of a document was missing; the suspect set of papers was handed to the bench, and ultimately somebody noticed that slip one was not numbered and that Russell was reading the figure 2 on the second slip through thin paper. 'Who cut off this piece of the letter referred to yesterday?' Russell asked. Le Caron answered: 'I did. It was to remove Mr Anderson's name because I did not want to bring him into the case.' 'I think it a pity you did,' Russell remarked. He demanded to see the page which Le Caron had torn off while sorting out the papers in Cork Street. 'Do you want to risk the lives of these men, Sir Charles?' the witness asked. Russell, seizing the chance to assert his status, flared up. 'Don't ask me questions, sir. The judge will see it before I see it. I shall not read anything that the judge does not permit.'

This episode, reported in the American press, was the basis of a rumour in Fenian circles that one of the names concealed was Dr Patrick Cronin's.

Russell later made a request for an order of the court permitting him and his learned friends to see all the documents from which Le Caron and Houston had culled their evidence. He must have known that this could not be granted; if all the defending counsel were to have access to secret documents, they could not have been kept from the two Irish Members of Parliament and Michael Davitt, who were defending themselves. Sir Henry James opposed the application in the interest of third parties, and Russell parried by suggesting that Sir Henry should go through them and tell him what was relevant. Sir Henry, who had earlier seen Le Caron indicate the height of the stack, protested: 'Well, I think that is the least acceptable proposition that could be made to me.' The President, showing an increasing aversion to the wealth of documents produced, observed: 'There would have been another still less acceptable proposition, and that is that the Court should do it.' Eventually it was agreed that Russell and James should examine the documents together.

In the intervals between this skirmishing, Russell endeavoured to assert the respectability and high professional status of leading V.C. members. In killing a man, he suggested, Alexander Sullivan had acted as a husband defending his wife from an insult. Le Caron agreed that Sullivan was well regarded as a lawyer, but he added that he did not move socially in the best Chicago circles. 'He was not unworthy of your society,' Russell commented ironically. Le Caron countered with: 'He was very useful.' Russell then went on to establish that when Parnell and Dillon toured America they were met by leading citizens, their meetings were often chaired by mayors, and that Parnell addressed Congress. Not denying this, the witness still insisted that the VC manipulated the tour.

Newspapers reported that, after his passages with the formidable cross-examiner, the witness remained as imperturbable as ever. After court hours, it was remarked, he moved about London freely and fearlessly.

At some time during the intervening long weekend—Friday to Tuesday—James and Asquith (Russell had foisted the dreaded job on to him) were shown the piles of over a thousand documents which the defence had been so anxious to see. They did not let the task burden their weekend. It must have been apparent that Le Caron's claim that he and Houston had spent ten working days on them was no exaggeration. James 'took some samples', as he put it, and referred them to Asquith. The two gentlemen came to the conclusion that the production of the papers they saw would not advance the interests of justice and would introduce the private matters of persons not concerned with the inquiry. Russell seemed to suffer no disappointment at the non-appearance of any further evidence, and the Court was doubtless relieved at being spared further readings.

The fashionable ladies, who had caused such surprise to the journalists accustomed to working in the sombre atmosphere of the law courts, were again present in substantial numbers and not a seat was vacant. If the great advocate was to break the witness it would have to be that day. The Commissioners, usually punctual, entered nearly ten minutes late, as if to heighten anticipation.

Russell again endeavoured to demolish Le Caron's story about his interview with Parnell. He affected surprise that the witness had recorded no memorandum on so important a matter, that he had never written to Parnell or O'Kelly to say how his mission was progressing. Le Caron said he had made a report personally, immediately after the interview. He was referring to his visit to Anderson, but Russell ignored this answer; he was trying to get his quarry on the run. 'Will you answer my question, sir! Did you make any report in writing?' Le Caron answered laconically in the negative, offering no information. One reporter remarked that 'The Major allowed the astonishment to express itself through three or four further questions'. Then, asked why he had not written to Parnell, he said: 'Because I had received my instructions where to write and to whom to write.' 'From whom did you receive your instructions?' Russell demanded. 'From Mr Patrick Egan,' Le Caron replied. 'Oh!' Russell exclaimed, raising his voice and assuming a severe expression. 'We must have this out! Have you told us one word of this up to this moment?' 'No,' Le Caron said coolly. Russell snapped: 'Why?' A burst of laughter in the Court greeted Le Caron's calm reply: 'I was never asked.'

Le Caron had had his revenge for the times he had been told that he was there only to answer questions. The laugh was on Russell, and he was unaccustomed to witnesses who scored off him. His bluff had been called, from then on his questions had no discernible thread, and he finished his cross-examination abruptly an hour and fifty-five minutes after he had started. Russell was also appearing that day in a turf libel case (as were James and Mr Lockwood, QC, MP) and was probably relieved to get away.

Mr R. T. Reid, QC, MP, representing other members of the Irish Party, took up the questioning. He occupied much less time than Russell had, and he tried none of the 'Will you answer my question?' and 'Let us get this straight' tactics. He returned to the subject, already raised by Russell, of Le Caron's remuneration, and was told that for the first three years he had received 'not one cent' and that over the years when he got allowances from the British and Canadian Governments he had paid out more in expenses than he had obtained. 'Your utility in that particular direction is at an end now,' Reid remarked. 'Have you made any arrangement, or got any understanding as to what is to be done for you?' 'I have not, sir,' Le Caron replied. On being asked whether he had been present at meetings when dynamite was discussed, Le Caron said that he was a delegate. 'Did you vote for dynamite?' Reid inquired. The answer raised another laugh: 'I was always on the side of the majority.'

Lockwood, for the Irish Party, caused some bewilderment by confusing the open meetings of the Land League with the secret conventions of the VC, so that for a time he and the witness were speaking at cross-purposes. This counsel—perhaps finding too sudden the switch from horse-racing scandals in one court to Irish-American intrigues in another—established nothing of significance.

During the re-examination by the Attorney-General, Le Caron produced a signed photograph of Parnell, explaining that he did not know whether it was the one Parnell had handed him or the one he had received by post. The Attorney-General wanted to give Le Caron an opportunity to justify his conduct in taking the Fenian oaths, as Russell had prevented him from doing so in an earlier sitting, but the President, with an eye on the clock, observed: 'I think it is scarcely necessary to enter into that,' and Le Caron, bowing graciously, said: 'I accede to your wishes, my lord.' As Nannie had by now arrived with his papers, Le Caron was able to produce Devoy's letter of 24 June 1881 (see Chapter 17) as evidence that he had passed on Parnell's message. A dull period ensued, while the Attorney-General and Asquith disputed the authenticity of a report in the *Irish World* of a speech made by Parnell in America, but attention quickened when Le Caron described how the Chicago jury which acquitted Alexander Sullivan of murder was packed.

The questioning ceased abruptly after Le Caron had agreed with Reid that Sullivan had appeared on platforms in the United States with men of the highest respectability. A pause followed. Le Caron asked: 'Is that all?' No reply came from the bench. An usher touched him on the shoulder to indicate that he should leave the box. Le Caron was not going to leave on such a dying note, however. Reporters agreed that his departure was dramatic. He turned to the judges, bowed and said: 'I am much obliged for your courtesy to me. I have not meant to be impertinent but I did not know the rules of the Court. I know that I have overstepped the bounds, and I thank you exceedingly for the courtesy you have all shown to me.'

The Attorney-General said: 'You have nothing to apologize for, Major Le Caron.'

Was there, perhaps, a tinge of irony in Le Caron's apology? At times he had been shown something less than courtesy, and the leading advocate of the day had tried to browbeat him, but he had remained urbane and imperturbable. In all the hours when Russell had striven to force a retraction from Le Caron, he had succeeded on only one minor point: Le Caron had originally said that the whole of Parnell's tour had been manipulated by the VC, whereas, he agreed, his personal knowledge of the tour extended only to the western part and his statement about the eastern half had been based on what he had learned 'from inside'. The *Daily Chronicle* suggested that Russell had abandoned his cross-examination, with 'heaps of points' which he had not tackled, because he saw that it was useless to continue. The paper summed up Le Caron's performance in terms which must have made painful reading for Russell and his colleagues.

> 'The best witness I ever saw in the box,' the eminent solicitor [Sir George Lewis] for the respondents is reported to have said yesterday, 'but I should like to have had the handling of him myself.' That was when Major Le Caron's cross-examination was nearly concluded, and perhaps it did not say very much for some of the counsel in the case. But whether the quotation be right or wrong, there is no doubt the Major or Doctor Le Caron, or Beach, has made just this sort of impression upon the great bulk of those who have heard his evidence for five days.

The London correspondent of the New York *Herald*, who described Le Caron as 'more like a shrewd far-seeing Yankee than an Englishman', reported what the now famous secret agent said when asked about the danger he must be in.

> As to the danger in the future, I am prepared for anything that may happen. I have done what I thought right to do and I will bear the consequences. Where I shall go and what measures I shall take to protect myself against assassins is a subject on which I have the best reason in the world for keeping silent. It is needless, however, for me to say that I shall not settle in Chicago, nor shall I make a visit to Ireland.

On 14 February, in the presence of Asher Prior and his clerk, Frank White, Le Caron signed his last will and testament.

Landing at Liverpool, Nannie and the children were met by Major Nicholas Gosselin, who was then supervising port security, and escorted to accommodation in the London borough of Brixton.

24

The Odious Profession

If Russell's ego had been frayed by his encounter with the former draper's apprentice, it was restored to its normal grandeur by his triumph over the miserable Richard Pigott. The long-awaited letters, the ultimate evidence to accomplish the Irish leader's downfall, the possession of which had emboldened *The Times* to press its charges so relentlessly, had been produced. A tactical move postponed the appearance of Inglis, the handwriting expert. MacDonald, the ailing manager of *The Times*, and Houston were no match for Russell, who made them appear to have been perfunctory and irresponsible in testing the authenticity of the letters. The defence had acquired letters too—blackmailing letters unquestionably written by Pigott. Russell, having exposed Pigott as a rogue and now pursuing him as a forger, asked him to write several words. Among them was 'hesitancy', which Pigott—incidentally revealed as no meticulous journalist—wrote 'hesitency', a misspelling occurring in the letter Russell had selected as the most useful for his purpose.

When the Court rose on Friday, 22 February, Pigott appeared to be near collapse. On Saturday, at Labouchere's house, and in the presence of another prominent journalist, George Augustus Sala, he wrote a confession that he had forged all the letters. But this was not his final statement. He went back to Anderton's Hotel in Fleet Street, and from there he sent a message to a Dublin solicitor named Shannon, who had been assisting Soames for *The Times*. Shannon called at Anderton's that night and again on Sunday night. Pigott made a statement to him, which he confirmed by affidavit, in which he significantly amended his earlier confession. He alleged that he had made the admission to Labouchere under fear of a prosecution for perjury, and on a promise that if he confessed to having forged all the letters the prosecution would be stayed and £2,000 settled on his children. Now he held that he had not forged all the letters, but had procured some he believed genuine from a man named Patrick Casey. The remainder, he conceded, he and Casey had forged together.

Pigott failed to appear when the Court reassembled on the following Tuesday. Anderson, as head of the CID, was handed a warrant for his arrest. Scotland Yard officers tracked him to Madrid, and were actually in the hotel where Pigott was staying when he shot himself.

The handwriting expert's services were no longer required; no possibility remained of asserting the credibility of the letters, not even on the basis of the forger's amended confession. For the prosecution the exposure of Pigott had been a disaster. Parnell's followers and his numerous sympathizers were jubilant. Now it was *The Times* which was on the defensive. Many more witnesses were still to be heard. As one Parnell supporter graphically put it, on any day a crowd of Irish policemen were to be seen, lounging about in front of Soames's office, smoking cigars while waiting to give their evidence. After the great scene they would seem to have only walk-on parts. Using the customary abject legal language, the Attorney-General on behalf of the paper withdrew the letters and apologized.

With the letters gone, the prosecution still had Le Caron's testimony to what Parnell had said to him in the House of Commons. No admissions whatever were extracted from the two men concerned. Sturdy, emphatic and soldierly in his manner, O'Kelly insisted that he could not recall meeting Le Caron at the House of Commons. 'It is a transaction upon which I have absolutely no memory. That is to say, there is no trace in my mind of the occurrence of such an event. I am not therefore in a position to say that it never did occur, nor can I swear that it did not.'

Parnell, handsome although haggard, could not remember it either:

> I do not recollect either his name or his appearance; but I think it very possible I may have had an interview with him. I cannot recollect his name or his appearance at all. I have no recollection of

him until I saw him in this witness-box. . . . Frequently I have seen American gentlemen passing through. Beach or Le Caron might have been among the number. He would have had no difficulty in obtaining an interview with me if he had wished to do so.

He denied the truth of every word of Le Caron's account of their conversation. As to the alleged statement that he had long since ceased to believe that anything but the force of arms would ever bring about the redemption of Ireland, he said: 'I never said that and I never even thought it. In the worst period of coercion I never for one single moment doubted that the constitutional movement of our Parliamentary action would succeed in the end.' He denied making any communication, direct or indirect, with Dr Carroll, Sullivan, Hynes or Devoy in or after May 1881 or instructing Le Caron or anyone else to open up negotiations with the Clan-na-Gael. The signed photograph must have been obtained from somebody else. Before Le Caron's evidence he did not know that the Clan-na-Gael was a murder society and he did not know it now. He raised a laugh when, asked about his tour in the United States which Le Caron had said was organized by the Clan, he retorted that it was not organized at all; he described it as chaos and related feelingly how he and Dillon had been caused unnecessary journeying by being shunted backwards and forwards.

Parnell's followers and the Liberals now attempted to turn the prosecution's retreat into a rout. The attack was opened in Parliament on 1 March by Sir William Harcourt, the Leader of the Opposition. He asked Sir Henry Matthews, the Home Secretary, on whose authority Mr Robert Anderson handed confidential papers in his possession in his official capacity to a man calling himself Le Caron to be taken away by him and examined and used by Le Caron and Mr Houston.

Matthews replied: 'Mr Anderson's action in the matter referred to was without my cognizance; but, so far as I am acquainted with the circumstances of the case, he acted in accordance with what was due to the Special Commission.'

This was not quite the admission that Harcourt was after, and he persisted. 'Did the Commission direct Mr Anderson to hand over confidential papers to Le Caron through Houston?'

Matthews' answer: 'No, sir. I conveyed nothing of the kind,' gave Harcourt the chance to say: 'Then he handed over the papers without authority from the Commission or the Home Secretary.' Harcourt then took an action liable to cause a nervous jolt to any civil servant, by giving notice that he would call attention to Anderson's conduct on 'the Vote on Account relating to the Metropolitan Police' in 'handing over confidential documents without leave from the Secretary of State and its bearing upon his position as Assistant Commissioner of Police in charge of the Criminal Investigation Department'.

Four days later a Member named Cobb asked whether Le Caron's account of how he obtained the documents from Anderson was true and, if not, whether the Government would prosecute Le Caron for perjury. The Home Secretary avoided the obvious trick, and replied that as Anderson would appear before the Commission, he would await the result before taking any action.

The build-up of prejudice went on; some Members took to shouting 'Beach!' when the name Le Caron was mentioned. At a widely reported Liberal mass meeting at Lambeth on 19 March, Harcourt described the return of Le Caron's documents by Anderson as proof of the incompetence of the Government and in particular of the Home Secretary. Cheered on by excited supporters, sensing the surging crowd emotion, Harcourt declaimed:

> The confidential agent, the Commissioner of Police, the head of the Criminal Investigation Department goes and hands over to an informer and to the agent of *The Times* the secret papers of the Home Office without the consent of the Home Secretary. I should have liked to see a man in that position do such a thing under any of the predecessors of the Home Secretary. I know where he would have been today. It would not have been at Scotland Yard.

Houston's association both with Pigott and Le Caron was used by Harcourt to imply that they were all on the same level of moral depravity. During what journalists call heated exchanges in the House of Commons on the following day, the Home Secretary maintained that Le Caron was entitled to use his own documents as he wished, Harcourt declared that 'such scandals have never been known before' and he referred to Houston and Le Caron as 'those miserable wretches' with whom it had been the Attorney-General's misfortune to have to deal. Harcourt had forgotten, or he chose to ignore, the high opinions of Le Caron he heard in 1882 when he himself was Home Secretary.

Already accused as he was of improper behaviour, Anderson was provoked into a further breach of civil service practice by defending himself in the press. His excuse was that those of his acts now under discussion were apart from his official position as Assistant Commissioner of Police; they arose from the time when he was an adviser to the Government on political crime; to explain his conduct completely would amount to a disclosure of the Secret Service arrangements of that period. 'To me, personally,' he wrote, 'the disclosure would be intensely gratifying. It would, moreover, supply a missing chapter of uncommon interest in the political history of recent years.' At considerable length Anderson then related how in December he had warned Le Caron of 'the terrible risks and penalties he would incur by coming forward' and 'point-blank refused' to put him in touch with *The Times*. Anderson's concern was to refute Harcourt's frequently repeated suggestion that he had handed government papers to *The Times* and Houston; the papers had never been on a government file, he argued, he had handed them to nobody but Le Caron, and giving back letters to informants was not an uncommon practice. Here he added a sentence which shows the professional intelligence operator reproving his thoughtless and inexperienced critics:

> And this discussion may do good if certain parties on both sides of the Atlantic should learn from it that they may give information to Her Majesty's Government and receive remuneration for doing so, with the certainty that their secret will be as well kept as Le Caron's was, and that, if they like to make the condition, their communications will be treated as strictly unofficial documents and be returned to them at any time they wish to claim them.

It is perilous for a civil servant to be dragged into a public controversy. Even if the dispute does not end his career, echoes of it can plague him throughout his working life and beyond. Anderson was making a brave attempt to prevent that happening to him, but with his experience of government service in a delicate area he can hardly have supposed that he had heard the last of the accusations.

The publication of his letter on 21 March was accompanied by a

leading article commending Anderson's letter: 'For dignity of tone
and straightforward statement, it seems to stand out in striking
contrast with the combination of recklessness and shiftiness displayed
by his unscrupulous accusers.' Passions were running too high,
however, for dignity of tone to prevail. John Morley, Gladstone's
biographer, thought the letter 'one of the meanest, as well as one of
the most insolent documents ever written'.

The Times also reproached Harcourt for terming a 'wretch' a man
who for twenty years had faced danger every day in the service of
his country. Doubtless Sir Charles Russell read these passages. If
they influenced him at all, it was to inspire him, in his opening
speech for the defence early in April, to go even farther than
Harcourt.

It was the era of the great court-room dramas, when advocates
behaved like popular tragedians, grimacing, gesturing, raising and
lowering their voices, even affecting tears, appealing as much to
emotion as to reason. These performances demonstrated the astonishing stamina Victorians possessed. Russell had already had a strenuous
time examining witnesses before the Commission, and in between
dashing to other courts to appear in different cases. Now his speech,
spread over six days, lasted for nearly thirty hours. It was the ruthless
speech of an advocate, omitting inconvenient testimony, assuming the
rightness of allegations which he had failed to establish in cross-
examination, introducing irrelevances, but providing the court with a
masterly digest of the favourable evidence.

Understandably, his references to Le Caron were particularly
vicious, while he sweepingly exonerated organizations and persons
against whom evidence had been given, declaring that the Land League
was innocent of any connection with murders which had been mentioned and clearing Patrick Egan's character with this remark: 'Le
Caron's statements respecting him do not appear to be credited by
the American Republic which has recently appointed him as their
representative at Chile'. He dismissed the power of Clan-na-Gael.
Not in its origins an outrage club, it was little better than the rump
of the old Fenian party reduced in numbers and influence but
showing considerable activity.

A section—it must have been a comparatively insignificant section of
an insignificant body—committed themselves to the dastardly and

inhuman policy of dynamite. But the history also shows secret attempts, persisted in, on the part of the Clan-na-Gael to capture and control the open movement, and it also shows that those attempts absolutely and entirely failed.

Ignoring Le Caron's main achievement as an agent, the wrecking of the Fenian invasion of Canada, Russell concentrated on what had been a minor part of his work.

> I certainly cannot avoid expressing my opinion that Mr Le Caron has not shown himself to be by any means the important person he at first sight seemed to be, for in the whole of this voluminous correspondence extending over years which he has carried on, I find no single instance of any forewarning of the authorities here of any dynamite enterprise upon the part of any single person mentioned; not as to Gallagher, not as to Mackey Lomasney—I think that was the name— not a single forewarning note of any attempted dastardly enterprise of that class, and I confess the impression borne in upon my mind by the consideration of these voluminous despatches of the V.C. is that that body appeared to spend a good deal of time in writing very long, and what I must call rubbishy conventions, and then tearing them up again.

Although Russell had failed to show in his cross-examination that Le Caron had pursued his perilous career for money, he now branded him as a mercenary spy.

> Here we have a man about whose odious profession I will not waste breath in talking. Surely the state of society has something faulty in it when the employment of such a man as Le Caron can be defended or can be necessary. His life was a living lie. He was worming himself into the confidence of men presumably honest, however mistaken in their views, only to make money and to betray them.

Reading at length from documents sent by Le Caron (when Russell used that name he sometimes added 'or Beach'), he represented that the whole story as shown in the 'long-winded secret circulars' demonstrated the very reverse of an alliance between Parnell and the physical force men. The Government of the day would have been glad of evidence to connect Parnell with illegal activities. Despite the importance Le Caron attached to the interview, he made no written report, nor had he communicated subsequently with Parnell or O'Kelly; no record had been produced that he had seen any of the persons, except for Devoy, whom he said he had been asked to see. When the libels in 'Parnellism and Crime' were written, Le Caron was unknown to the agents of *The Times*, and he was only the *deus ex machina*—or should he say *diabolus ex machina?*—who came forward disgusted at the weak manner in which the case was being presented, to save it from ruin and collapse.

Houston was denounced by Russell as the 'tempter', whose offers of money led Pigott to produce the forgeries. Brought up in Dublin, he must have known Pigott's character; behind him was a conspiracy, the Loyal and Patriotic Union, representing the landed interest of Ireland, a class arrayed against Parnell. According to the pro-Parnell *Daily News*, Houston 'changed colour and looked as if he were trying to swallow a lump in his throat'.

Russell did not spare his personal friend Soames or his former clients, the *Times* management. 'Mr Soames, a respectable professional man, seems to have allowed his partisan feelings to blind his judgement.' *The Times* had made an inadequate withdrawal concerning the letters and was guilty of culpable recklessness in omitting ordinary precautions to test their genuineness. 'The key to the whole fabric of calumny that lifted up its head under the name of "Parnellism and Crime" was a want of common charity, a want of common care, a neglect almost criminal, and an attitude of mind which endorsed and accepted the gravest accusations against political opponents.' Although Russell did not mention John Woulfe Flanagan by name, his references to the paper's leader-writer must have been galling because they were patronizing: 'a young man—I am sorry to say an Irishman' who seemed to possess some literary ability which might have been better employed than in defaming his countrymen and degrading his country's cause, but 'it is due to him to say that he was after all the machine, the creature of those who paid him'.

Having dealt with the evidence for so many hours, most men would have been hoarse and desperately tired, anxious to cease talking and sit down, but Russell went on to a peroration, in itself a lengthy and powerful speech on the Irish situation, to call the court's attention ('very briefly', he remarked apologetically) to the accused men's motives. Two classes existed in Ireland, he said, the majority of the people and the governing minority. 'It is a system as completely centralized and bureaucratic as that which rules in Russia and governs Poland, and which was to be seen in Venice under Austria.' He had spoken, he declared, not merely as an advocate but for the land of his birth.

Almost at the end he turned on *The Times* again. 'This inquiry, intended as a curse, has proved a blessing. Designed, prominently designed, to ruin one man, it has been his vindication. In opening this case I said that we represented the accused. My lords, I claim leave to say that today the positions are reversed. We are the accusers; the accused are there.' Russell pointed.

'One almost pitied the accusers,' wrote the *Daily News* representative, 'as they sat, in sulky meekness, under the lash.'

In his final words, 'delivered in a tremulous and broken voice', as a reporter observed, he expressed the hope that the inquiry 'will remove grievous misconceptions and hasten the day of true union, of real reconciliation, between the people of Ireland and the people of Great Britain; and that with that true union and reconciliation there will be dispelled, and dispelled for ever, the cloud, the weighty cloud, that has rested on the history of a noble race and dimmed the glory of a mighty empire.'

The applause was such that the ushers took some time to restore silence.

No one on the defence side could complain of 'a lame presentation of the case', but the Clan-na-Gael, so lightly brushed aside by Russell, was soon to provide a reminder of the realities.

25

The Clan Strikes

'I rise under terrible strain, because after the disclosures of Major Le
Caron in London the organization as an organization is no more.'
Andrew Foy, a member of Camp 20 in Chicago, was taking part in
what an onlooker described as 'a pretty warm discussion' caused by
local newspaper reports of the Parnell Commission. A heresy hunt
was starting; Foy demanded that every member with the faintest
taint of suspicion should be expelled. A Captain Thomas O'Connor
pointed out that Le Caron was a paid agent of the Clan's executive
body—'a parcel of rogues' who had squandered $100,000 'to send
our best men across to England to have them put behind bars'.

Camp 20 (known to the public as the Columbia Club) heard some
no less shocking revelations from a member who had been visiting
another camp where Dr Patrick Cronin—impatient because the
Clan's trial committee was withholding the report of its proceedings
—leaked the serious evidence he had given against the Triangle. He
reported Cronin's charges that Alexander Sullivan had mis-
appropriated funds and betrayed the dynamiters. The Senior
Guardian, John F. Beggs, came to his close friend Sullivan's defence
in a tirade in which he threatened to stop these attacks even at the
cost of shedding blood. Beggs appointed three of the brothers,
Daniel Coughlin (a detective in the Chicago police), Martin Burke
and Patrick O'Sullivan to deal with the menacing situation.

While the trio worked diligently on their brief, the Parnell
Commission was still pursuing its deliberations. The culmination of
their planning in Chicago came at about the time when Sir Charles

Russell in London was asserting Alexander Sullivan's respectability and scoffing at the idea that the Clan-na-Gael was a murder club.

During the latter part of February Cronin was kept under observation from rooms rented for the purpose across the street from his lodgings in Clark Street, Chicago. The plotters decided that he must be lured away from there. Burke, calling himself Frank Williams, in March hired a cottage about an hour's drive distant, furnished it sparsely and also moved in a large trunk, a valise and a long strap. Then he left. The cottage adjoined premises occupied by Patrick O'Sullivan's ice business.

In April O'Sullivan, accompanied by a lawyer, visited Cronin with a contract for his workmen's medical care. It was a strange request because the ice trade was not dangerous, no workmen had ever been injured, and doctors in the vicinity of the cottage were available. The unsuspecting Cronin signed. On leaving O'Sullivan gave the doctor his business card; the arrangement was that if an accident occurred when O'Sullivan was out, someone else would call Cronin by presenting the card.

After an evening meeting of Camp 20 on 3 May, Burke and another man occupied the cottage. During the following day Coughlin visited a livery stable to order, 'for a friend', a horse and buggy to be ready at seven o'clock. Some time afterwards he telephoned O'Sullivan to go out. The ostler subsequently recalled that the man who came objected that the horse was white and the buggy had no side curtains, but nothing else was available.

The stranger drove to Cronin's address, presented O'Sullivan's trade card, told the doctor that O'Sullivan was out of town, and begged him to come urgently to a man with a crushed leg. Cronin picked up his bag and some cotton and was driven hastily away.

Cronin's disappearance was still unknown in London when the Attorney-General, looking over the evidence to the Commission, came upon the idea that this determined opponent of Alexander Sullivan might be induced to appear as a witness. Stating that the information was required by Arthur J. Balfour, the Chief Secretary for Ireland, William Henry Joyce approached Le Caron for an assessment of Cronin. Writing under the alias of J. R. Howard, Le Caron expressed the view that Cronin might be persuaded, 'for a money consideration', to appear if by doing so he could pose as a true friend of the Irish cause by exposing the corruption of Sullivan's administration. He appended his opinion of Cronin: 'For years past I have known him to be a professional scoundrel and a liar of the Millen type and I would not take his word or trust him one inch. My relations with him have always been *outwardly* friendly. . . . He is an egoist of the first water.'

Le Caron was now under police protection. Two burly Irish policemen were stationed at the Great Western Hotel in London to guard a man registered in the name of Mr Holland. The duty worried them. A busy hotel presents an impossible problem for security men; ideally, to protect a threatened individual, they would like to reserve an entire corridor and the rooms above and below him. One entrance to this hotel is in Paddington station; passengers, then as now, came off trains every few minutes and could walk unhindered into the hotel and the bar.

Any informed observer must have rated their charge's chances of survival as negligible. He was a distinctive-looking man, wearing no disguise, whose features were familiar from newspapers and magazines; the false name would not have delayed a determined assassin for long. The Irish Republican Brotherhood disposed of ample men and resources. Five years earlier the British authorities had secured a report showing that in Great Britain alone the Brotherhood numbered 11,500 members (2,500 of them in the south of England) and in Ireland there were 36,000. These numbers would not have diminished significantly. In every organization the majority of members are passive, but those thousands would certainly have included some willing killers. An even greater threat could have come from the United States. Luke Dillon, then 41, the dynamiter who escaped undetected to the United States after explosions at the Junior Carlton Club and the House of Commons, planned to track Le Caron down. According to Detective-Inspector John Sweeney, writing in the habitual style of policemen, 'reports had come to hand' that the Clan-na-Gael intended (he claimed to quote their own phrase) 'to put his lights out'. Shortly after Mr Holland registered there, men asked at the hotel's reception desk for a man of that name. Probably they were journalists who by devious ways had got on his trail but the policemen could not risk waiting to see whether they produced guns or notebooks. The receptionist and the porters were instructed to show nobody up.

Detective-Sergeant Patrick McIntyre, of Scotland Yard's political department, was on royal guard duty at Osborne, on the Isle of Wight, when he was ordered to return to London. Queen Victoria feared assassination and was heavily guarded; possibly McIntyre was selected as an experienced Fenian-spotter on the principle that if anything happened to Anderson's agent Scotland Yard could claim that it had done its best.

Following briefing at headquarters he asked at the Great Western Hotel for Mr Holland. A suspicious porter, after some delay, fetched a large Irishman, who satisfied himself as to McIntyre's identity before ushering him into a sitting room, where he was introduced to Le Caron. When the Irish guards learned that they were to hand their notorious charge over to the detective, they did not conceal their relief.

No cordon of the type that existed at royal residences could be maintained around this vulnerable man, so the first task was to remove him to a more private place. McIntyre had the bulk of Mr Holland's cases moved to the left luggage office at Euston station, to put pursuers off the scent. He and his companion left not by the street entrance but by the door leading on to the station concourse, and went to private lodgings in Marylebone Road, where they apparently fixed themselves up very comfortably. *The Times* (according to McIntyre) allowed them £20 a week for expenses, and allocated a further £9 a week for Le Caron's dependents, who were accommodated in lodgings as far away as Brixton so that their association should not be apparent. They could scarcely have enjoyed peace of mind but they were free of financial worry. Rumours circulated that the paper had, for the sake of Le Caron's family, taken out an assurance policy on his life; if this was true, the premium must have been substantial.

Le Caron's part in the Parnell Commission was over but as, during his mornings of leisure, he read *The Times*, he saw frequent mentions of his name as the key witness. On some days, in Number One Probate Court, the chief issue seemed to be his credibility. He also learned from the paper that Cronin had been murdered.

26

'So Much Abused'

After Le Caron's evidence, Pigott's suicide and Sir Charles Russell's speech, the level of excitement in the Parnell Commission's proceedings subsided, but many of the allegations in 'Parnellism and Crime' were still not dealt with and numerous witnesses were yet to be heard. Such zeal was exercised by the prosecution in rounding up witnesses that, as John Morley wrote, 'so varied a host was never seen in London before. There was the peasant from Kerry in his frieze swallow-tail and knee-breeches, and the woman in her scarlet petticoat who runs barefoot over the bog in Galway. . . . Men who had been shot by moonlighters limped into the box, and poor women in their blue-hooded cloaks told pitiful tales of midnight horror.'

November had arrived when Sir Henry James began his closing speech on behalf of *The Times*. He was less emotional than Russell and his appeal was to the judges rather than to the spectators in court and the public outside. Near the opening he emphasized the importance of Le Caron's evidence.

'My lords, who is this man on whose evidence much depends in this case, on whom I have to ask you to rely, whose work I ask you to accept? As far as I know, that man's character, apart from anything that took place in America in connection with his conduct towards the Clan-na-Gael, is unimpeached.' After relating how Le Caron was recruited as an agent, James asserted that from the time he was asked to obtain information down to the present:

. . . he had been playing the part of the interests of this country
alone. It is true that he did from time to time take the promissory
oath of those who were plotting . . . not only the open and more
healthy warfare of the field, but plotting assassinations, the destruction of the life and property of innocent people. And for
twenty years that man has held his life in his own hand. He never
could have had one moment's security, one moment of certain
repose. One letter miscarried, one person unfaithful to his trust in
the post office, one accident any hour occurring, and that man's
death in a moment was as certain as any person's death must be as
the ultimate result of life.

James then referred to that awkward subject of Le Caron's taking
the Fenian oaths. On whose behalf were complaints of his oath-
taking made, he asked. Was it of the assassins who required secrecy
to avoid the punishment which would follow their detection? Here
he turned on those Irish Members of Parliament 'who find it
convenient to take one day an oath of allegiance to an Irish republic
and endeavour to secure it, and the next day take the oath to be true
to their sovereign'.

A detective, James continued, was praised if he apprehended a
criminal after a crime.

Why then should the conduct of this man be condemned? Here
you have a man who, running such risks as probably no human
being ever ran before, occupied himself with defeating crime
before it was carried out, and sought to prevent the consequences
of awful crime, and thus to save the lives of those who had no other
protector. This man, detective as he may have been, has thwarted
the machinations of men who are not fit to be regarded as belonging
to the human community. Is he, I ask, to be attacked because he
has wrought this good?

Quoting Russell's condemnation of Le Caron's 'odious pro-
fession', James argued that Le Caron had been employed by men of
high honour, seeking to protect the country. Men who refused to
avail themselves of information about the attack on Canada or the
blowing-up of public buildings would be 'accomplices, almost par-
ticipators in the dreadful deeds that would be perpetrated'.

James pointed out, in a tribute to 'the witness who has been so much abused', that the authenticity of the documents produced by Le Caron had never been questioned, that correspondence confirmed that Parnell had entrusted him with messages, that the visitors' book of Kilmainham Prison proved his visit, and that except for Parnell no witness had contradicted his evidence.

Counsel in the case seem to have felt that a peroration predicting a bright future for Ireland was obligatory. James's was shorter and less eloquent than Russell's, but showed no greater prescience:

> . . . the truth being told, it must be that a people, stirred by an awakening conscience, will be aroused from the dreams of a long night, and when awake they will despise their dreams. They will seek new modes of action with true men to guide them, and then it will be—God grant that it may be—that blessings will be poured on a happy and a contented people.

The applause was muted compared with the reception accorded to Russell's oration. A brief silence followed, as if no one could grasp that the Special Commission, unique in British legal history, would meet no more. With comparatively few expressions of impatience, the judges had listened for 128 days to the testimony of 450 witnesses (including 30 informers), to numerous speeches of inordinate length, to 98,000 questions and answers, and to the reading of wearily repetitive documents. Now Sir James Hannen spoke a few words of thanks for the assistance the Court had received, the three judges bowed to counsel and withdrew.

The Commission was, for the time being, out of the news, but the Clan-na-Gael was not. The trial of those accused of murdering Cronin was nearing its end and the story was being eagerly followed, as it had been since the spring, by newspaper readers in the United States, Canada and Britain.

A woman passer-by had seen a buggy drawn by a white horse pull up outside the cottage adjoining O'Sullivan's premises; a man alighted and hurried inside. Burke was known to be there already. Coughlin, driven by a man identified as John Kunze, arrived later and entered the cottage. During the night policemen saw three men, sitting on what they took to be a tool chest, in a waggon in the neighbourhood of Lake Michigan. A blood-stained trunk with traces of cotton was found near the lake on the morning of 5 May. Fifteen days later, the lease of the cottage having expired, the landlord and his wife entered their property; the walls were splashed with blood, the carpet gone, the floor roughly repainted, and an arm wrenched off a rocking chair. The trunk key lay on the floor; the valise was missing. They told the police. Within two days the doctor's naked body, battered about the head, was found in a catch-basin by workmen cleaning the sewers. The victim's clothes, packed in the valise, were recovered some months afterwards from a sewer.

Immediately on the announcement that the corpse had been identified Burke fled to Winnipeg, where he bought a ticket to Liverpool. Before he could leave Canada he was caught.

Suspicion fell on Alexander Sullivan as the instigator, and a coroner's jury returned a verdict of wilful murder against him. He was arrested but released for lack of evidence—his second escape from a murder charge. Before Beggs, his committee of three, and Kunze could be put on trial, seven weeks elapsed during which 1,115 citizens were put up for selection as jurymen.

The State Attorney, sketching the background to the crime, made what was in effect an indictment of the Clan-na-Gael. Cronin's papers, seized by the prosecution, included the trial committee's minutes with the case he had presented against the Triangle. A wider public than ever Cronin could have reached learned of the misappropriation of huge sums, of the abandonment of the arrested dynamiters, and the scornful neglect of their dependents. The assassination, and the revelations of the Clan's secret operations, provided 'perfect corroboration', Le Caron claimed, of his evidence to the Parnell Commission. *The Times*, remarking that it was the State Attorney's 'cue to paint Dr Cronin as an innocent and patriotic Irishman, murdered by the hands of villainous rivals', pointed out that Cronin and his associates did 'not condemn the Triangle for dynamiting, but for dishonest dynamiting', and it added this judgement: 'Both wings of the Clan-na-Gael were engaged in the same devilish plots, and while every one must rejoice that the assassins even of a dynamiter should meet their lawful doom, Cronin merits no more sympathy as an individual than "Captain Mackey" himself. He was brutally murdered, while himself engaged in plotting the wholesale murder of others.'

Le Caron and *The Times* made their point but, with the extensive publicity given to its ruthlessness, the Clan had made its point too, and more effectively than had the merely verbal accusations of its opponents. What was in the jurors' minds when they acquitted Beggs? The Senior Guardian's subordinates, Coughlin, Burke and O'Sullivan, were given life imprisonment; accustomed to regarding their operatives as disposable, the leaders would not have thought that a heavy price. For his part in driving the buggy, Kunze (not a member of the Brotherhood) was sentenced to three years. The white horse—so intense was public interest—became a celebrity and, with less exertion, earned the livery stable more than the three dollars charged for the hire on the night of the murder by being exhibited in a 'dime museum'.

27

Scramble in the Corridor

Considering the nearly 8,000 pages the transcripts of the evidence covered, the Commission's report—a Blue Book of 120 pages with 40 pages of appendices—appeared speedily. The news that it was to be available at 10 p.m. on 13 February 1890 in the Vote Office at the House of Commons caused (according to *The Times*) 'a scene of almost unparalleled excitement in the lobby', and when the porters were seen approaching with bundles 'the expectant members raised a cheer and excitement rose very high'. A slight delay occurred while a porter struggled to open the Vote Office door. In that moment an impatient member cut the string of one of the bundles with a penknife and the gentlemen scrambled for the copies scattered over the corridor floor.

The terms and the style of the report hardly justified such desperate eagerness. The judges were unanimous and cautious; they gave no sign of having been moved by Sir Charles Russell's survey of Irish history and description of rural misery. After the exposure of the forged letters it was inevitable that Parnell should be exonerated on the accusation of insincerity in denouncing the Phoenix Park murders, but on other charges their pronouncements still left room for much argument. They decided, for example, that the respondents did not directly incite persons to the commission of crime other than intimidation, but they did incite to intimidation, and the consequence of that intimidation was that crime and outrage were committed by the persons incited. This was not quite the total exculpation or condemnation which the Members, feverishly turning over the leaves as midnight approached, had been hoping for.

The strong attacks on the principal witness for *The Times* had failed to impress the judges. They referred to him not as Beach but as Le Caron, they accepted the substance of his interview with Parnell at the House of Commons, and they quoted in full Devoy's acknowledgement, dated 24 June 1881, of Le Caron's letters conveying Parnell's desire that Devoy should come to Europe and offering to pay his expenses. Their conclusion was contained in these two paragraphs.

> We think that these passages tend strongly to confirm Le Caron's testimony; and we come to the conclusion that Le Caron has given a correct account of the message he was requested by Mr Parnell to convey to Devoy.
>
> Mr Parnell denies that he ever said that he had long since ceased to believe that anything but force of arms would bring about the redemption of Ireland; but he bases his denial on the fact that he never thought so. It is, however, not impossible that in conversation with a supposed revolutionist Mr Parnell may have expressed himself so as to leave the impression that he agreed with his interlocutor.

The report, the *Spectator* commented, 'will be quoted as conclusive in favour of its own view by each of the parties in the great contest'. This proved to be so, and it was true of their supporters in the press. Commentators analysed each paragraph, interpreted whether it favoured Parnell or his accusers, and then totted up the score. The *Pall Mall Gazette* and the *Daily News* hailed the report as a complete acquittal of the Irish party. The *St. James's Gazette* thought the opposite: 'The Commissioners indicate that they believe Le Caron. It follows that they do not believe Mr Parnell.' The *Standard*, urging that nothing was to be gained now by a state prosecution, remarked: 'The offenders have already been judged guilty by a competent tribunal.'

'I am inclined to join in the chorus of conditional satisfaction with which that long-laboured document has been received by all the parties most interested and concerned,' wrote Michael Davitt in the *Nineteenth Century*. Davitt, who represented himself before the Commission and was complimented by the presiding judge on the ability with which he did so, made a striking comment on Le Caron as a witness.

The credence given by the Commissioners to Le Caron's whole story—his history of Clan-na-Gael doings and the account of the alleged conversation and interview with Mr Parnell—is one of the marked features of the Report. It is significant proof of what a skilfully played part can do in the way of making a good impression upon men who are supposed to be influenced only by the hard facts of evidence. As a witness, and apart from what he swore, Le Caron was the very best put forward by *The Times*. His manner in the witness-box could not be improved upon. Deferential, but not obsequious, to the Court; attentive and courteous to Sir Charles Russell, resourceful in his replies all round, and entirely devoid of bravado, except when he loudly boasted of always having been 'an English-born fellow', he succeeded most artfully in masking the character and career of a spy behind the well-acted personality of a patriotic Englishman who for near thirty years had risked his life in efforts to counteract the plans of England's enemies. It was an histrionic performance of a high order, and would have won any jury of Englishmen into a sympathetic belief in the artist's romantic recital—especially as the Clan-na-Gael were not in court and could not therefore unfold a counter-story. Le Caron's testimony was against absent enemies. The stage was all his own, and right good use he made of it.

Davitt queried whether the letter quoted in the report was really by Devoy; he accepted that Le Caron did have an interview with Parnell but thought the substance of it highly improbable; he considered it significant that Le Caron did not write to Parnell about the success of his mission; he contended that the sealed packet contained only a letter of introduction; he claimed that the circulars read to the Commission were all in Le Caron's handwriting; he disputed the accuracy of Le Caron's recital of persons present at Clan-na-Gael conventions; and he denied that the Clan had captured the National League.

The Times published a letter from Le Caron on 5 March 1890 without revealing his address. Le Caron wrote that Davitt 'very prudently abstained from examining me in the box', and he observed that if Anderson had been called as a witness the record of the interview with Parnell would have been forthcoming. Le Caron then gave, for the first time, the information that not all his documents had been returned to him.

It is urged that only one 'single instance' of corroboration, and that the Devoy letter, was furnished the Commission of the later stages of investigation. It will be interesting, though I question if it will be pleasant news to Mr Davitt and his friends, to learn that the most important part of the correspondence between Devoy, Sullivan, Hynes and myself was forwarded to the Government at the time, and that the different documents now form part of the official records of the Home Office. When, on the eve of my appearance in the witness-box, I applied for them, I was informed they had been made official, and their use was absolutely denied me for this reason.

The letter of introduction from Devoy to Egan, Le Caron went on, may or may not have been in the sealed packet. 'Had the letter been an open one, as Mr Davitt states, and not the sealed document I have sworn it to be, I would be better able to speak regarding it.' Davitt's statement that all the circulars read to the Commission were in his handwriting was false, Le Caron concluded; about half were the original printed papers, and the others were copies because the originals had to be returned.

In the House of Commons, on a Government motion to accept the report and an amendment by Mr Gladstone asking the House to record its reprobation 'of the false charges of the gravest and of the most odious description', Members indulged in a repeat in miniature of the Commission's proceedings. The debate, which dragged on for six days, was less decorous than the proceedings in the Law Courts, speakers being frequently interrupted by applause or objections. The six counsel engaged in the Commission got into a wrangle in which they employed the same passages they had declaimed in court, causing one Member, Howorth, to observe: 'It is a painful thing to witness these conflicts between members of a noble pro-fession.' *The Times*, which had been reserved in its handling of the report, interjected comments on the previous night's speeches; when Asquith said, yet again, that Le Caron's information had not pre-vented one single explosion, the paper remarked in a leading article: 'This is just as if a man should argue that sanitary improvements are of no use because no one can point to the fever they had saved him from. The fact that the police were put on the alert would prevent, and undoubtedly did often prevent, the conspirators from making any attempt to carry out their wicked designs.'

The debate ranged over the now familiar topics—the Clan-na-Gael, Parnell's visit to America, the alleged take-over of the National League, Patrick Ford and the *Irish World*, the Skirmishing Fund, the Land League, the Jubilee Plot, the Phoenix Park murders, Pigott's forged letters—in no special order and often with no discernible thread. Speakers frequently used the vocabulary of Victorian melo-drama—evil, villainous, monstrous, despicable, dastardly—and held the floor for, apparently, as long as they pleased. Pigott, Houston, John Woulfe Flanagan and Anderson were all attacked as Irishmen unworthy of the name, but the Opposition's most bitter attacks were concentrated on Le Caron. That the judges had believed the man Beach's account of his interview with Parnell aroused particular fury. 'No, I reject that as the invention of a liar!' declared Mr H. Fowler. Thomas Sexton, who as Lord Mayor of Dublin had met Le Caron in that city, made the strongest attempt to discredit the witness. He announced that some letters had been handed to him with a view to his communicating them to the House. One, which he read, was dated 3 April 1886 when there was a labour dispute on the South Western Railroad. Addressed to T. V. Powderly in his capacity as leader of the Knights of Labour, it was purportedly signed by Le Caron; the writer, suggesting that a peaceful strike would achieve nothing, asked to be put in touch with 'a few of your lieutenants' to whom he would supply explosive materials to destroy 'every bridge and culvert on the road'.

The impact of this reading must have been highly gratifying to Sexton and his colleagues; it caused a gleeful uproar on the Opposition side. But a challenge soon came from the Chief Secretary for Ireland, A. J. Balfour, who asked: 'Why did the honourable gentle-man read that letter to the House when it could not be made the subject of cross-examination, when it could not be looked at? Why did he not bring it before the judges—it was written in ample time—in order that Le Caron's evidence if false might be blasted by this reference to Le Caron's previous action?'

In a subsequent exchange Sexton repeated that the letters had been handed to him in the last few days, Balfour protested that they had not been available for examination, and a Member who inter-jected the suggestion that the documents were forged was cheered. Sir William Harcourt said that the letter, 'if it be true, shows that Le Caron is a criminal of the deepest dye', and remarked that the letter incriminating Parnell had not been subject to cross-examination.

The Times took up the argument, following Balfour's line that the letter 'had been in existence three years at a time when Le Caron's examination before the Commissioners was causing intense excitement both in this country and in America, and when such a document would have been a most potent weapon in the hands of Sir Charles Russell. . . . '

A prompt denial, dated 11 March, came from Le Caron in a letter to the paper:

> I beg to state that the letter alleged to have been written by me to Terence V. Powderly, late member of the Clan-na-Gael executive, a copy of which was read last night in the House of Commons by Mr Sexton, is a pure fabrication; and I respectfully defy and challenge the production of this, or any other communication, written or signed by me addressed to that individual.

Members on the Government side might have been more worried than they were about the alleged existence of a document revealing Le Caron's role as an *agent provocateur* if Sexton had not also claimed possession of a letter marked 'Private' from the Prime Minister, Lord Salisbury, to Pigott. Such an improbability scarcely needed refutation. Another denial came from William Henry Hulbert, author of *Ireland Under Coercion*, who rebutted assertions about himself made in Sexton's speech and added: '. . . as an active member of the Democratic Party of the United States, I know that Major Le Caron's statements as to the relative influence and importance of the different sections of the Irish movement were strictly correct.'

Sexton did not produce the letters and nobody answered Le Caron's challenge. Parnell took no part in the debate. Gladstone's amendment was defeated and the report adopted.

Writing over the initial 'D', a correspondent called attention in *The Times* of 15 March to a Clan-na-Gael rule reproduced in the Commission's report: 'S.Gs. shall in their sound discretion or by direction of the F.C. have power to publish information calculated to deceive the enemy.'

'D' added: 'The enemy is England.'

Three years had elapsed since *The Times* published its first article on 'Parnellism and Crime'. In that period the paper's fight against

Home Rule and the supporters of Irish independence had been unceasing. Now, although the editorial policy was unchanged it had to bear the costs of what was at best an indecisive campaign. Because of the constitution of the Commission, which put the paper in the position of prosecutor, and the judges' decision to hear the evidence on all the charges, *The Times* had to foot a bill of over £200,000—an immense sum at that time. A comparatively minor item was the settlement for £5,000 of Parnell's libel action in Scotland. The business was to be financially crippled for years, but no less serious was the damage to the paper as a national institution. To its readers it had been the ultimate authority on every matter of public concern, from the intentions of the German Emperor to the correct spelling of a place-name, and now it was shown to be fallible in (to borrow one of its favourite phrases) a matter of the utmost gravity. Opponents had been handed a single word to clinch all arguments; Members of Parliament and hecklers at public meetings took to shouting 'Pigott!' when *The Times* was quoted. Readers had also turned to other journals not through disagreement with its views but because its news suffered by the almost verbatim coverage of the Commission's proceedings which *The Times*, both as a paper of record and as a participating party, felt obliged to supply. When an issue had to carry both that report and the Parliamentary debates, little space remained for general news, and this at a time when the scope of daily journalism was widening and penny papers (*The Times* cost three-pence), brighter in style and presentation, were providing competition.

In the clamour about the forgeries the fact that most of the other charges had not been refuted (as they were mostly based on Fenian sources they could not be denied anyway) was obscured. No prosecutions followed and Parnell was not brought down; the management at Printing House Square must later have reflected bitterly that the Irish leader had been heading for a crash without any nudging by them. The flow of funds from America was not checked. If Le Caron wondered whether the sacrifice of his anonymity had been worth the result, he never revealed his thoughts.

28

A Detectives' Delight

Not everybody accepted that the mystery of the Parnell letters was solved. Pigott, it will be recalled, revoked the confession, made under pressure at Labouchere's house, that he had forged all the letters. In a second statement, he declared that he had procured certain letters he believed to be genuine from Patrick Casey, although he admitted that he and Casey had forged some together. Anderson considered the second confession more likely to be true than the first. Like Inglis, the handwriting expert, Scotland Yard investigators thought the signature was Parnell's. It could have been written on a blank sheet for a clerk to write a letter on the other half. Anderson's conclusion was that the text was written by Arthur O'Keefe, a sub-editor on William O'Brien's paper, *United Ireland*, who helped Parnell with his correspondence while they were both imprisoned in Kilmainham; the motive was not to assist the Unionists but to commit Parnell to a more extreme policy. If this were so, it explains how paper supplied to the Dublin Land League came to be used.

John Walter, the proprietor of *The Times*, never conceded that the letter was forged, and his view was shared by a well-to-do female relative who was anxious, even at that late stage, to prove that the paper had not been wrong. She turned to the arch-spy in the same spirit as Conan Doyle's characters sought the aid of Sherlock Holmes. Hitherto Le Caron had not been involved in this unfortunate episode. He may have acted out of gratitude for the paper's financial support; otherwise, it is surprising that he allowed himself to be tempted, especially as the assignment involved a trip to Paris where so many Fenians had put themselves beyond the reach of the British law. Houston, still smarting from his humiliation, was the other spirit animating the mission. Officially Scotland Yard wanted nothing to do with the project; the allegations made during the Commission's hearings that government resources were used to assist *The Times* were still in the public memory, but Houston approached Anderson for permission to take Le Caron's police escort with them. Always impatient of bureaucracy, Anderson agreed so, delighted at the prospect of the trip, and apparently not doubting his capacity to foil assassins, Detective-Sergeant McIntyre went with them.

Some preparation was made for their reception in Paris; Mr W. Graham, one of the barristers who appeared for *The Times* before the Commission, was already there. After Houston, a Presbyterian, had been to church to pray for the success of the mission, the first move was to meet Patrick Casey, one of the men who escaped after the attempt to rescue Ricard Bourke from Clerkenwell Prison. He and his brother Joseph (tried and acquitted after the attack on the police van in Manchester in 1867) were working as compositors on the European edition of the New York *Herald* and active in a group of Irish exiles.

McIntyre told the story in two short paragraphs in a newspaper article. He promised a fuller version when he wrote his book of reminiscences, but that work never appeared, and Le Caron and Houston remained silent about the expedition. Doubtless they were under some constraint, and the questions raised by their trip are not answered. What was Le Caron's part intended to be after he had abandoned his cover? Why should Patrick Casey—unless well remunerated—have been expected to help *The Times*? British agents had penetrated the Fenian organization in Paris, and possibly McIntyre owed to them the information at which he could only hint. It is evident that the set-up was a detectives' delight. According to McIntyre, Casey suggested bringing a John Hayes from America, and Hayes was trailed from New York by two Pinkerton's men hired by a section of the Clan-na-Gael on the supposition that he was inquiring into matters connected with the murder of Cronin. Hayes, it turned out, was really a British Government agent. Joseph Casey was reporting all this to Michael Davitt, who passed the information to Members of the Irish Parliamentary Party, one of whom communicated it to Soames, the *Times* solicitor. 'It is difficult for me to make clear to the readers the exact position of all the parties in this game,' McIntyre wrote despairingly.

Whatever all this information was that circulated so widely and no doubt so profitably to so many people, it did not serve to establish the genuineness of any Pigott letters. John Walter's loyal and trusting relative must have blanched when she saw the bill.

The two detectives, McIntyre and Detective-Inspector Sweeney, shared the duty of looking after Le Caron. With Sweeney posing as Dr Simpson and Le Caron as Dr Howard, they lived in suburban hotels, moving from time to time. From his background Sweeney might well have taken a different path and become a Fenian. In 1859, when he was 2, his father had been evicted from his small farm in County Kerry, but this painful experience did not turn the family against authority. Young Sweeney's ambition was to join the Royal Irish Constabulary because he admired their smart uniform, but when he was 16 his parents moved to London, and his father became a foreman at a market garden near Earls Court. At 18 the son joined the Metropolitan Police. Like his colleague, he enjoyed his charge's company and admired him, thinking that 'he was bound to rise somewhat in whatever walk of life he selected'.

Sometimes Le Caron abandoned his alias as when, accompanied by a Scotland Yard man, he visited his relatives in Colchester and his presence was announced in the local paper. He had long talks with the famous preacher, C. H. Spurgeon, who had known his father, and explained the Fenian philosophy to such effect that Spurgeon changed from a Gladstonian Liberal to a Liberal Unionist. Le Caron, however, was less open to conversion, and the man who could move huge congregations failed to shake his visitor's scepticism.

That cool courage, which enabled him during the Parnell Commission to move freely about town, was gradually replaced by caution. Sweeney noted that on their journeys 'he was certainly a good deal frightened. Especially at railway stations he would go peering anxiously about, fearing that anyone he saw might be his enemy. If he saw the same man twice in one day he would insist that this stranger must be following him.' It can be presumed now that he was in the early stages of what was to prove a fatal illness.

As time receded, and no attempts were made on his life, Scotland Yard thought that he could be reunited with his family. They all moved to Sunnyside, Eliot Bank, Sydenham, described by the appreciative Detective Sergeant as 'a fashionable house' where 'we lived for some time in first-class style'. The house is no longer there, but the immediate area is still a pleasant place; the road known as Eliot Bank winds up a gentle incline among mature trees and residents enjoy a view across London. The area was much favoured by prosperous City men; it was within carriage drive of their offices, if they were very grand, or they could conveniently travel the six miles by rail. The policemen found the family life most agreeable, and no doubt the presence of a daughter who (as Sweeney recorded) 'distinguished herself by winning a prize at a beauty show' added to the amenities of their unusual assignment.

Always a prolific writer, Le Caron now wrote his memoirs. The life story of a mysterious character who, as every newspaper-reader knew, had passed unscathed among assassins and dynamiters, but who still lived in hourly danger, was bound to sell. *Twenty-five Years in the Secret Service: the Recollections of a Spy*, published in 1892 by William Heinemann at the rather stiff price of fourteen shillings, enjoyed a considerable success and went on selling for some years after the author's death.

In a sense, the book is a postscript to his evidence before the Parnell Commission: he asserts his veracity ('one unalterable characteristic will apply all through, and that will be the absolute truthfulness of the record'); he pays tributes to Anderson ('a kind trusty friend and adviser, ever watchful in my interests, ever sympathising with my dangers and difficulties') and McMicken ('ever ready and willing to help me, meeting me at a moment's notice, placing everything at my disposal, and watching over my safety and my interests with a fatherly care'); and—recalling that Gallagher was carrying £1,400 and Monroney £1,200 when arrested—he criticizes the Government's parsimonious attitude to the Secret Service.

The narrative contains an error which is surprising in view of his sharp memory and the magnitude of the occasion: he records the second Fenian invasion of Canada as taking place in April instead of May, although his description of the weather during the operation is more suited to the late spring.

Of himself, apart from his espionage, he reveals little. The reader learns nothing about whether he liked Gilbert and Sullivan operas, whether he saw Mrs Langtry as Rosalind in *As You Like It* or Charles

Hawtry in *The Pink Dominos*, or who were his favourite authors. The only indulgence to which he admits is that of smoking sixteen cigars a day. It is clear that he had no need to turn to intelligence work to earn money. His ability to do well from overt activities made him independent and gave him the best cover he could have; his Secret Service employers required no such expedients as setting him up in a sham business.

If his motive was not the simple patriotism he asserted it to be it is difficult to explain his dedication over such a long period; any initial thrill at being a secret agent would not have survived acquaintance with the reality. He does not reflect on 'the Irish question', although he claims to have done so with the 'poor deluded Irish in the States' who put up the money:

> . . . to discuss with them the eternal subject of Irish nationality is to respect their honesty of purpose, no matter how much we feel called upon to condemn their methods of procedure. But, for the blatant loud-voiced agitator, always bellowing forth his patriotic principles, while secretly filling his pockets with the bribe or the consequences of his theft, there can be no other feeling but that of undisguised loathing.

He devotes only a few lines to his oath-taking, which the Commission prevented him from explaining. 'True, I had to take many oaths. But what of that? By the taking of them I have saved many lives.'

29

'Almost Superhuman'

The family, with their attendant detective, moved from Sydenham to 11, Tregunter Road, South Kensington. Guarding Le Caron was no longer the problem it had been but it was less fun for the policemen who had enjoyed their trips, because his health was failing. Eventually he was confined to bed. Operations for appendicitis were not then performed if the patient had fever, and one of the symptoms of the condition is a high temperature. A local practitioner, Dr S. F. Harvey, called in Gilbart Smith, a Harley Street consultant. Anxious to adduce evidence on his agent's behalf, Anderson records that the specialist became a warm 'Le Caronite' and quotes him as saying: 'I became increasingly impressed by his very remarkable respect for the truth.' Anderson was a frequent caller, and to Le Caron's quiet amusement (increasing weakness did not turn his thoughts to religion) he prayed in his presence.

Le Caron's temperature did not subside, no operation was performed, peritonitis set in, and he died at home on Sunday, 1 April 1894, aged 52 years and 6 months.

Fenians in Britain and America suspected that the report of Le Caron's death was a trick to deceive would-be assassins. As Devoy remarked, 'There were undoubtedly many men ready to kill him if they could only find him, and there was general anger among Irishmen that he had been allowed to escape.' Certainly the Clan-na-Gael had been less efficient in its vengeance than it proudly claimed, and if Le Caron were alive it still had a chance to redeem its reputation. The rumour that Le Caron was merely in hiding was quashed by Ralph Meeker, London representative of the New York *Herald*, who had covered the Parnell Commission. Through Scotland Yard he obtained permission to see the body, and he reported that the famous spy was indeed dead.

Devoy gave vent to his anger in an interview in the Chicago *Sunday Times* of 8 April 1894. Speculating on Le Caron's fate beyond the grave, he complained that 'with twenty millions of a race that hates informers as does no other in the world supposed to be thirsting for his blood not a hostile hand is raised against him, and he dies peacefully in his bed . . . the champion spy of the century'. Although in his earlier acquaintance he seems not to have observed Le Caron's racial inferiority, he now described him as having 'dark hair, sallow complexion, and long nose, all doubtless due to a strong strain of gypsy blood, which is common around Colchester', and years later he referred to 'Beach, the half-breed Gypsy spy'. (Devoy was to call Eamonn De Valera 'the half-breed Jew who split the unity of the Irish Race'.) For 'the prince of spies', as he once termed Le Caron, no condemnation could be strong enough; he quoted with approval 'a Fenian obituary' pronouncing him 'a disgusting moral monster'.

In contrast, an anonymous contributor to the *St. James's Gazette* raised his father's status to that of 'an English gentleman living in the eastern counties' who, in passing his son's letters to the Home Office, had acted 'as any wise and sensible Englishman would do'. Recalling that the family name was Beach, this writer thought there was

> . . . perhaps one reason why those who were his well-wishers should restore to this brave and alert servant of the country his true English surname, for Major Le Caron was an Englishman through and through. . . . How a man who had gone through Major Le Caron's experiences could have emerged with a manner so excellent, a mind so simple, and a character so unspoiled, it is difficult to imagine. For years he had been brought into close contact with the vilest scum of the created earth, the Irish-American-Fenian-whisky-saloon-bosses, who were the mainstay and support of the Irish party in the United States.

The *Essex County Standard* hailed him as 'a native of Colchester, whose extraordinary and unique career will render him undoubtedly one of the historic personages of English history in the 19th Century', and, reviewing his activities, observed that 'during his early life in Colchester probably none suspected what dormant energies fraught with the vastest importance to this whole Empire were in train for development'.

'Few men have served their country at a more terrible personal risk than Major Le Caron, and have received less recognition for the faithful performance of a dangerous and thankless task,' wrote the *Daily Graphic*, which went on to refer to the controversy surrounding him. 'The world uses the term "spy" as one of reproach. But mines can only be met by countermines, and conspirators can only be baffled by the use of such men as Major Le Caron.' The paper summed him up as 'one of the most remarkable men of modern times . . . perhaps the most daring spy that ever lived'.

The ethics of espionage occupied a columnist in the *Illustrated London News:* 'How far a man may practise the profession of a spy for patriotic motives, and yet conform to the code of honour is a nice question for casuists. Most people will continue to regard the professional spy with a certain repugnance; but the merit of rare courage, coolness, and audacity cannot be denied to Henri Le Caron.'

The Times, which had so faithfully acknowledged its obligation to him, recalled the fate of Dr Cronin as showing the unremitting danger in which Le Caron had lived.

This deadly peril, nevertheless, he faced, and faced successfully, for a quarter of a century. There is something almost superhuman in this spectacle of a man who could devote his life to so terrible a duty, keeping his secret locked up from all companions except his devoted wife. The self suppression which enabled him to come through such a lifelong ordeal would alone entitle him to respect. It must not be forgotten that the risks he ran were not ended by his return to this country. From the moment he took his place in the witness box he was liable to become the object of a murderous conspiracy, and the danger arising from this cause could only be evaded by a further life of secrecy. Whatever may be the verdict of posterity upon his life Le Caron was a remarkable man. And if the exigencies of the public service require the services of a spy to track down those who are plotting murder against innocent people, by a parity of reasoning it is difficult to maintain that such a career as Le Caron's is not justified. He was a 'military spy' who deliberately and conscientiously took up a vocation and carried it out with astonishing courage, perseverance, and success.

The death certificate, issued in Kensington, London, on 2 April 1894, incorrectly states his age as 51. It is the kind of discrepancy on which Sir Charles Russell would have pounced with a snarl of 'Let us have this out!' His occupation is given as 'Major in Army (United States) M.D.' and the cause of death as 'Typhlitis (recurrent) 3 years Exhaustion', certified by S. F. Harvey MRCS. His daughter May reported the death.

Information about the funeral arrangements was restricted to avoid public interest. The cortège left Tregunter Road at 12.30 p.m. on Saturday, 7 April, and arrived at Norwood Cemetery at two o'clock. A service was conducted in the cemetery chapel by the Anglican chaplain, the Revd Hugh St Maur Willoughby; the pretence that the family were Roman Catholics had been abandoned on their arrival in England. The weather was fine, but cloudy, with a light east wind, as the mourners stood at the graveside. Accompanying his widow and children were his mother, his brother and an aunt and uncle. Of the other mourners, the only names mentioned in the brief press accounts were those of Soames (who brought a wreath from *The Times*), Houston, William Heinemann and Dr Harvey. A large floral cross was inscribed 'To our darling father', and there was a wreath from Paris bearing a card which simply read: 'From his old friend'. Presumably the sender was the man who befriended him during his early days in Paris.

Norwood Cemetery contains costly and elaborate memorials to famous and prosperous Victorians; once familiar names meet the eye along the main avenues. That week Lord Hannen, who as Sir James Hannen presided over the Parnell Commission, had been interred there. Le Caron, who always voted with the majority, has a modest position—plot 25795–86—in the second tier from a path. To mark the grave Nannie chose a stonemason's design which is well represented in the locality: a four-foot marble cross round which is carved a trailing grape-vine. The inscription reads: IN LOVING MEMORY OF HENRI LE CARON. DIED APRIL 1ST 1894. AGED 51. 'THY WILL BE DONE'

The cross has now fallen and lies among the coarse grass covering the plot.

It is fitting that after such a career mysteries should remain. Why is his age wrongly recorded on the death certificate and the grave? Possibly his family never saw his birth certificate—when in America he would not have kept among his papers a document revealing his real name—but they would surely have read his autobiography where, in the first chapter, he discloses in elaborate Victorian style that 'A faded entry in the aged records of the ancient borough of Colchester evidences the fact that a certain Thomas Beach, to wit myself, came into this world some fifty and one years ago, on the 26th day of September 1841.' Did his daughter May, distressed and confused on the day following her father's death, simply suffer a lapse of memory when reporting to the Registrar, and did the family, for consistency's sake, keep to this figure when instructing the undertaker and the stonemason?

A secret agent's finances are bound to be obscure, and Le Caron's enemies could safely make public assertions about his wealth in the knowledge that no confirmation or denial would come from official quarters. In America he lived, to all appearances, as a prosperous professional man, but in 1870 when the invasion of Canada had taken him away from his medical practice he was so short of cash that he could not buy a winter coat. During the following seventeen years his reporting on Fenian activities took much less of his time and he could devote himself to his practice and building up commercial interests. Claims that he was offered inducements by the Government or *The Times* to leave America and appear as a witness before the Parnell Commission are unsubstantiated; Anderson tried to dissuade him from doing so and Printing House Square had never heard of him. It is possible, however, that he still had a credit with the Government. At Nannie's suggestion he did not take his grant as a lump sum but asked Anderson to dole the money out to him when he needed it; according to Anderson, Le Caron drew only half.

When he made his will in 1889 he was a man of some substance. He bequeathed to his wife the then very large sum of £5,000 and his effects, and £20 each to his brothers and sisters. Nannie was to sell his personal assets, to invest the sums realized in government or real securities in England, and to use the income for her maintenance and that of their children until the youngest reached the age of 21. His stipulation that the securities should be bought in England may reveal an assumption that Nannie would not take her family back to the United States or it may simply express his faith in British financial stability.

He made only one alteration to this will. Two years later, in a codicil dated 24 March 1891, witnessed by George Newman, a provision merchant, and his attendant police officer, John Sweeney, he revoked—without comment—the legacies to his brothers and sisters.

Now comes the surprise. The grant of probate, registered on 3 August 1894, recorded his personal estate as £523 7s. 6d. No duty was paid. No other information about his finances is available. Official records relating to his estate have been destroyed in the course of time.

Le Caron was not the kind of man to make a boastful gesture by bequeathing money he did not possess. Throughout their married life Nannie shared his confidences; she knew what work he was doing and what his income was. In the five years between his making his will and his death over £5,000 became officially unaccounted for. Did the codicil to his will imply that he saw his assets dwindling and feared that his estate would be inadequate to pay out these small legacies? Was so much money drained away by the cost of living in England without an occupation (except that of writing a book) and, later, by doctors' bills? This seems improbable. Detective-Sergeant Patrick McIntyre, who for periods lived virtually as a member of Le Caron's household, wrote that Nannie and four children were brought to England at the expense of *The Times* and that they and their police escort were thereafter maintained by the paper's management. The fact that *The Times* has today no record of these payments does not mean that they were not made. It is true that in the early 1890s Printing House Square was suffering from the financial drain of the Parnell Commission, and the disbursement of large lump sums is unlikely, but newspapers have a tradition of liberality with money for special purposes and the support of the famous spy and his entourage could well have been 'lost' in the petty cash. Alternatively, a government department handling secret funds could have prevented publication of the amount of Le Caron's assets and transferred the money to wherever Nannie needed it.

Victorians would also have suspected another possibility—that bags of sovereigns had been hidden under the invalid Le Caron's bed. Speculation about his estate went on, even though a good many hostile investigators must have felt frustrated when they saw that modest figure on the grant of probate.

Whatever she inherited, Nannie took it and her family back to the United States, not to Braidwood where the former members of Camp 121 would scarcely have welcomed them as neighbours, but to her home state of Tennessee, where, thirty-two years earlier, she had released the captured soldiers from the log smoke-house and, two years after that, 'scampered the plains' with the happy-go-lucky cavalry officer.

30

A Loud Echo

Sixteen years after Le Caron's death Sir Robert Anderson KCB, then nearly 69, revived the old controversy about his handling of secret documents by writing a reminiscent article in *Blackwood's Magazine* of April 1910 entitled 'The Lighter Side of my Official Life'. It was a discursive piece, containing such retired civil servant's jeers as '. . . the "red tape" element in Government work is exasperating to any one who has a soul above trivialities' and 'Though I was never censured when in the wrong, I was occasionally censured when in the right.'

Anderson was no doubt an irritating and opinionated man, inclined—as pious people are—to maintain that an action was morally justified because his principles debarred him from committing an immoral one. But incidents in his career, when he was publicly attacked by men who were actually aiming at a larger target, must have rankled. Sir William Harcourt had criticized him openly about his method of dealing with Le Caron's reports and then privately written him a placatory letter; yet Sir William was in no position to lecture Anderson as he himself retained in his personal possession secret documents he had acquired as Home Secretary. Anderson was not alone among intelligence officers in making his own decision about the disposal of documents. E. G. Jenkinson, who compiled the memorandum presented in 1885 to the Cabinet on the Clan-na-Gael, destroyed his secret material when he resigned a year or so later. Experience ought to have taught Anderson to lie low but (like Le Caron) he could not keep quiet about his secret work.

No public controversy would have been aroused by his article in *Blackwood's* but for what he later called 'a passing reference': 'To the present hour I do not know whether the Home Secretary was then aware of my authorship of "The Times" articles of 1887 on "Parnellism and Crime", for in relation to that matter I acted with strict propriety in dealing with Mr Monro and not with the Secretary of State.'

Time had not dulled Nationalist Irish Members' fury at the part played by Anderson's famous agent in the Parnell Commission. Now they saw a chance to take their revenge on Anderson and to give a new airing to old issues. Two of them promptly (on 11 April) called attention in the House to Anderson's admission.

Asquith, the Liberal Prime Minister, whose Government depended for its majority on Irish Members' support, and who as a young barrister had represented Parnell before the Commission, was emphatic in his comment: 'I cannot use language sufficiently strong to express my condemnation of the admitted breach of official duty of which Sir Robert Anderson was guilty.' Four years later Asquith's views on the preservation of official secrets seem to have softened: in letters to Venetia Stanley, thirty-five years younger than himself, with whom he was in love, he repeated the substance of Cabinet discussions and quoted secret despatches from Sir John French, then commanding the British Expeditionary Force, to Lord Kitchener, the Secretary of State for War; but in 1910 he was all for a strict observance of the rules, at least as applied to civil servants.

What the Nationalist Members had in mind was then revealed. John Redmond asked for information about Anderson's pension (part of it was paid under the Police Vote and part by the Home Office) and requested facilities 'for pressing the desirability of ending his pension'.

Anderson rushed a letter to *The Times* with such speed that it appeared in the issue of the 12th. It was, in essence, an appeal to the Prime Minister to release him from his obligations of secrecy so that he could state his case. He confessed to 'unfeigned distress' at the Prime Minister's censure, argued that the exposure of the Jubilee dynamite plot was 'a public service of such magnitude that in view of it any breach of official propriety might be condoned', and repeated his statement of 1889 that the Fenian pamphlets he had then quoted were not Home Office papers but the property of his informant.

No reply came from the Government but after a week the attack was renewed in Parliament by Irish Members who tried, unsuccessfully, to inquire about the allocation of Secret Service funds and how it was that Anderson, on his retirement in 1901, received a knighthood. T. P. O'Connor, the Nationalist Member for the Scotland division of Liverpool, moved to reduce the Civil Service Commission vote by £900, the amount of Anderson's pension.

By now James Monro, aged 72, had intervened. The two men had been estranged after what Anderson called 'a most painful incident' (apparently caused by Anderson's mentioning his *Times* articles) just before Monro resigned from the Chief Commissionership in 1890. Was Monro, in writing what Anderson called 'an amazing letter', continuing that row? He could have been exhibiting the civil servant's instinctive dive (even after retirement) for cover at the prospect of a controversy, displaying jealousy of that knighthood (his decoration was a CB, awarded in 1888), resenting the credit claimed by a former subordinate, or (as Anderson diplomatically maintained) falling victim to simple forgetfulness. He might merely have desired to establish the truth. It was one man's word against another's, and Monro must have been gratified by the degree of acceptance his denial found and the resulting jibes to which Anderson was exposed.

Winston Churchill, the Home Secretary, read Monro's statement to the House:

> In 1887 I was Assistant Commissioner Metropolitan Police under the Home Office, in charge of secret work. Mr Anderson was an agent of mine (as were others), chiefly as being a channel of information received from a man in America, who corresponded directly with him, and whose name I did not know. When the *Times* earlier articles appeared, they certainly caused a sensation in London and everybody was talking about them. . . . As a matter of fact, no such authority was asked by Mr Anderson, and none was given to him by me. . . . A long time afterwards, Mr Anderson informed me that he had written one or more of the articles, and I felt much annoyed.

Then, as now, the House laughed immoderately at the simplest witticisms. An ebullient Irish Member, Mr Macveagh, interjected: 'Then the statement of Sir Robert Anderson that he had official permission to write these articles is another edition of Anderson's Fairy Tales.'

The hilarity increased at Churchill's response: 'I don't think I could have expressed it better than the honourable gentleman has done.'

Ostensibly the debate was about a former civil servant's alleged breach of the rule forbidding contributions to the press. Anderson certainly came in for a good deal of abuse as an Irishman unworthy of the name and as a 'miserable underling', but the speeches ranged over *The Times*'s anti-Parnell campaign, the setting-up of the Commission, the alleged use of government resources to support *The Times*, and Le Caron's reward. Macveagh claimed to know that Le Caron was paid £10,000 for his evidence. Balfour, the only survivor present of the Cabinet at the time of the Commission, justly remarked: 'It is really an attempt to reopen the controversy which shook this House and shook the country only a quarter of a century ago.'

Churchill joined in the mêlée by deploring the idea of a Commission to investigate matters which could have been dealt with by the courts. Returning to the original subject, he was cheered as he declared that Anderson had broken a Treasury rule forbidding officials to write for journals without permission, any infringement of which rendered a civil servant liable to instant dismissal, and the cheers grew louder as he went on to put Anderson in his place by observing that the articles in *Blackwood's* were written in a style of gross boastfulness, in a style of 'how Bill Adams won the Battle of Waterloo', and the authorship of 'Parnellism and Crime' was, after twenty-three years, 'only now revealed by the garrulous and inaccurate indiscretion of advancing years'.

Expert as they were at disrupting Parliamentary proceedings, the Irish Nationalists took to shouting down speakers who opposed a reduction in the Civil Service Commission Vote and the debate petered out in uproar.

Despite the severity of their strictures, the Prime Minister and the Home Secretary did not favour depriving a long-standing civil servant of his pension. The majority supported them by 164 votes to 94.

Anderson continued to enjoy his pension until his death on 15 November 1918. During that period he added five more religious works to the fourteen he had already published; the title of the last, which appeared in 1916, was *Misunderstood Texts of the New Testament*.

Asquith was the last person to give an eye-witness's impression of Le Caron in the witness-box. 'Some of us', he said during the debate, 'will never forget that most remarkable and most sinister personality.'

Sources

NEWSPAPERS

Chicago Sunday Times, Daily Chronicle, Daily Graphic, Daily News, Essex County Standard, Gleaner (Huntingdon), *Globe* (Toronto), *Herald* (New York), *Irish World, Morning Post, New York Times, Ottawa Citizen, Ottawa Times, Pall Mall Gazette, St James's Gazette, Standard* (London), *The Times, Tribune* (New York)

PERIODICALS

Blackwood's Magazine, Contemporary Review, Essex Review, vol. III, *Gaelic American, Graphic, Illustrated London News, Nineteenth Century, Spectator*

ARTICLES, BOOKS AND OFFICIAL DOCUMENTS

Anderson, Sir Robert, *Sidelights on the Home Rule Movement*, John Murray, London, 1906

Anderson, Sir Robert, *The Lighter Side of My Official Life*, Hodder & Stoughton, London, 1910

Central Criminal Court Depositions, CRIM.1/27

Clarke, Thomas J. (alias T. James), *Glimpses of an Irish Felon's Prison Life*, Maunsel & Roberts, London and Dublin, 1922

Colonial Office files, Canada, May 1870, CO 42/686

Creighton, Donald, *John A. Macdonald*, 2 vols., Macmillan, Toronto, 1951, 1955

Curran, Charles, 'The Spy Behind the Speaker's Chair', *History Today*, November 1968, pp. 745–54

Devoy, John, *Recollections of an Irish Rebel*, Irish University Press, Shannon, 1929

Devoy, John, *Devoy's Post Bag, 1871–1928*, eds. William O'Brien and Desmond Ryan, 2 vols., C. J. Fallon, Dublin, 1948, 1953.

Dictionary of National Biography, Supplement, vol. 1, London, 1909

Jenkinson. E. G., *Memorandum on the Organization of the United Brotherhood, or Clan-na-Gael in the United States*, printed for the use of the Cabinet, 26 January 1885, CAB.37/14

Le Caron, Henri, *Twenty-five Years in the Secret Service: The Recollections of a Spy*, Heinemann, London, 1892

Lyons, F. S. L., *Charles Stewart Parnell*, Collins, London, 1977

Macdonald, John A. and Judge Gilbert McMicken: McMicken's reports to the Prime Minister from 1858 to 1889 are contained in the John A. Macdonald papers (MG 26 A) in the Public Archives of Canada, Ottawa

Macdonald, John A. (Capt.), *Troublous Times in Canada*, published by the author, Toronto, 1910

McMicken, Gilbert, *The Abortive Fenian Raid on Manitoba*, The Historical and Scientific Society of Manitoba, Winnipeg, 1888

Marlow, Joyce, *Captain Boycott and the Irish*, André Deutsch, London, 1973

Morley, John, *Life of William Ewart Gladstone*, Macmillan, London,. 1903

O'Broin, Leon, *Fenian Fever: an Anglo-American Dilemma*, Chatto & Windus, London, 1971

O'Broin, Leon, *The Prime Informer*, Sidgwick & Jackson, London, 1971

O'Broin, Leon, *Revolutionary Underground: The Story of the Irish Republican Government, 1858–1924*, Gill & Macmillan, Dublin, 1976

Parnell Commission, Report of the, London, 1890, pp. 103–5

Quinlivan, Patrick, and Paul Rose, *The Fenians in England, 1865–1872, John Calder, London, 1982*

Ryan, Mark, *Fenian Memories*, M. H. Gill & Son, Dublin, 1946

Short, K. R. M., *The Dynamite War*, Gill & Macmillan, Dublin, 1979

Sweeney, Detective-Inspector John, *At Scotland Yard, Experiences during Twenty-seven Years' Service*, ed. F. Richards, Alexander Moring, London, 1905

Times, The History of The, vol. III, The Times, London, 1947

Index

Index

Index